Oscilloscope Laboratories presents

A Werc Werk Works Production

in association with Telling Pictures and Rabbit Bandini Productions

A Rob Epstein/Jeffrey Friedman film

James Franco Howl David Strathairn Jon Hamm Bob Balaban

Alessandro Nivola Treat Williams with Mary-Louise Parker and Jeff Daniels

Casting by Bernie Telsey, CSA Music by Carter Burwell

Animation Designed by Eric Drooker Animation Producer John Hays Costume Designers Kurt and Bart

Production Designer Thérèse DePrez Editor Jake Pushinsky Director of Photography Ed Lachman, ASC

Based in part on *Howl and Other Poems* by Allen Ginsberg

Co-Producers Brian Benson Andrew Peterson Mark Steele

Executive Producers Gus Van Sant Jawal Nga Producers Rob Epstein Jeffrey Friedman

Producers Elizabeth Redleaf Christine Kunewa Walker

Written for the Screen and Directed by Rob Epstein & Jeffrey Friedman

OSCILL◉SCOPE

DOLBY DIGITAL
In Selected Theatres

HOWL

A GRAPHIC NOVEL

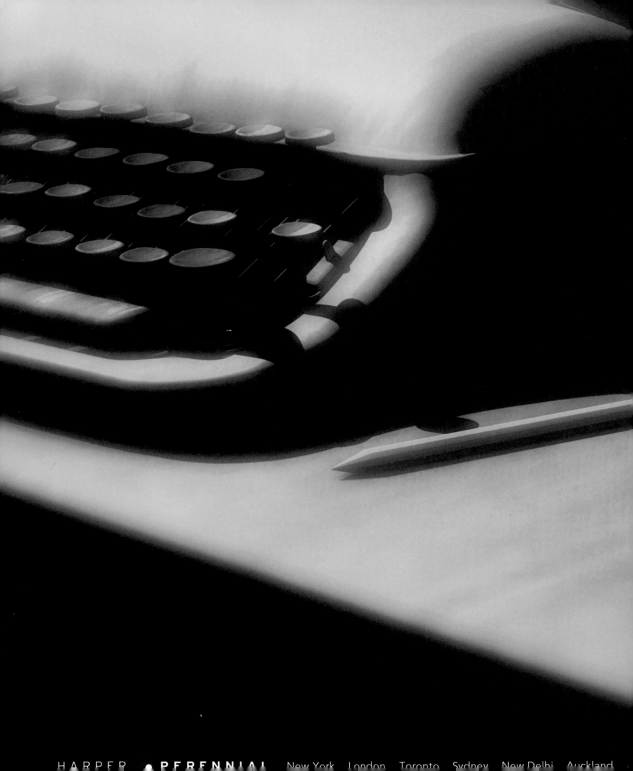

HARPER ● PERENNIAL   New York London Toronto Sydney New Delhi Auckland

HOWL

A Graphic Novel

Poem by Allen Ginsberg

Animation Art by Eric Drooker

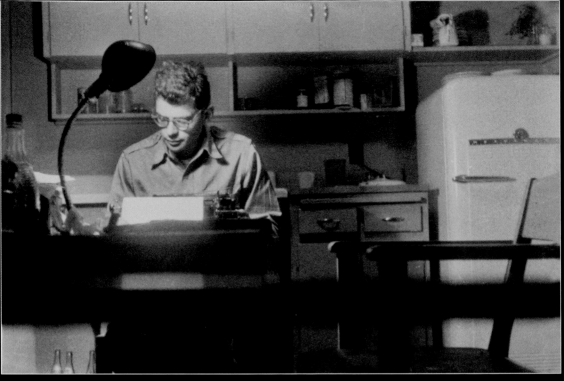

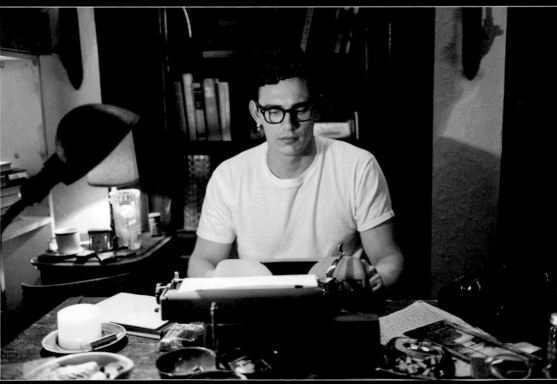

Top: Allen Ginsberg typing *Howl* manuscript,1955.   Bottom: James Franco as Ginsberg in the film, *Howl*, 2010.

HARPER ● PERENNIAL

Artwork in this book is from animation designed by Eric Drooker for the film *HOWL*.
Some of Eric Drooker's images were first published on covers of *The New Yorker*.

Special thanks to Rob Epstein and Jeffrey Friedman,
and to John Hays, who guided the animation process.

The poem "Howl" was first published by City Lights Books in 1956.
Read *Howl and Other Poems* and *Howl on Trial: The Battle for Free Expression*,
published by City Lights Books. When visiting San Francisco, please drop by
the City Lights Bookstore, "A Literary Meetingplace since 1953."
www.citylights.com

HarperCollins books may be purchased for educational, business, or sales promotional
use. For information Please e-mail the Special Markets Departement at
SPsales@harpercollins.com

FIRST EDITION

Cover and book design by Eric Drooker
www.Drooker.com
Photo of Allen Ginsberg on page 6 by Peter Orlovsky

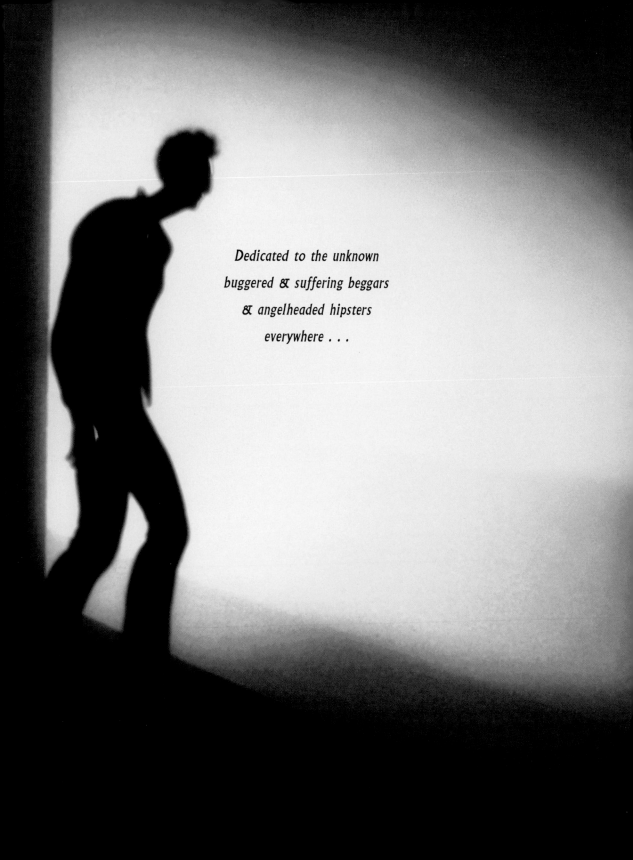

*Dedicated to the unknown
buggered & suffering beggars
& angelheaded hipsters
everywhere . . .*

Contents

DROOKER

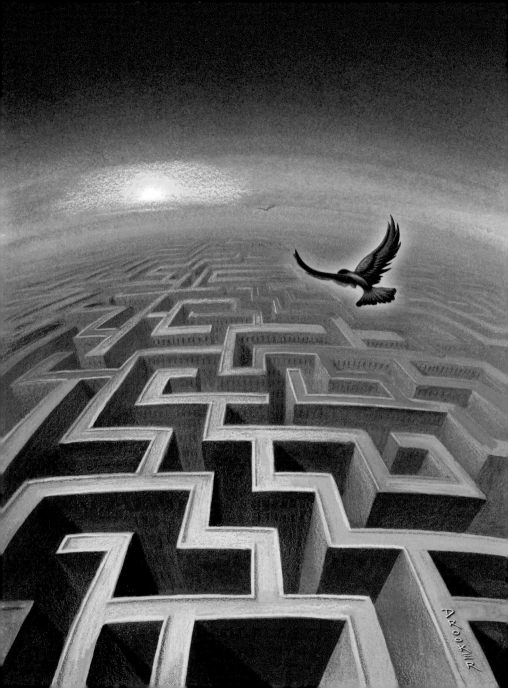

Introduction

First time I hung with Allen Ginsberg, one long hot summer night in 1988, the streets were hopping mad. Riot cops on horseback were slowly moving in our direction, enforcing a midnight curfew, but the chanting crowd refused to leave Tompkins Square Park—a refuge for punk, homeless, squatters, artists, and other riffraff who'd been "keeping real estate prices down" on Manhattan's Lower East Side. When the police charged, swinging clubs, we lost each other in the crowd.

When I bumped into Allen a year later, and he realized that I was the artist who'd created so many of the street posters in the neighborhood, he admitted that he'd been peeling them off brick walls and lampposts, and collecting them at home. He suggested we do a poster together. Over time, we collaborated on numerous projects, bouncing his words off my pictures.

Our book, *Illuminated Poems*, became an underground classic, and ultimately caught the attention of filmmakers Rob Epstein and Jeffrey Friedman. They were just starting to direct a feature film about Allen's early poem "Howl" and its historical significance—with Hollywood actors playing Ginsberg and his friends Jack Kerouac and Neal Cassady. When they approached me with the ingenious idea of animating "Howl," I thought they were nuts and said, "Sure, let's animate Dante's *Inferno* while we're at it!" Then they told me I'd work with a team of studio animators who would bring my pictures to life . . . how could I say no?

Last time I hung with Allen Ginsberg was on a cold winter night three months before he died. Over the phone he'd invited me to join him for dinner at his favorite Chinese restaurant. As usual, we discussed current events, politics, and eventually got on to the subject of art. Allen brought up the painting *The Triumph of Death* by the 16th-century master Pieter Bruegel the Elder.

"Have you ever seen it . . . *in real life?*" he asked.

"No . . . not yet. Where is it?" I asked.

"It's in Spain, in the Prado Museum. It's *enormous* and fucking *terrifying!*"

After supper we went up to his apartment, where Allen was in the process of getting rid of things he no longer needed.

"Hey, Eric, you want this jacket? It looks about your size."

He handed me a crimson-red blazer jacket. I tried it on. . . .

"Good fit," he said, "now it's yours."

—Eric Drooker

HOWL

for Carl Solomon

I

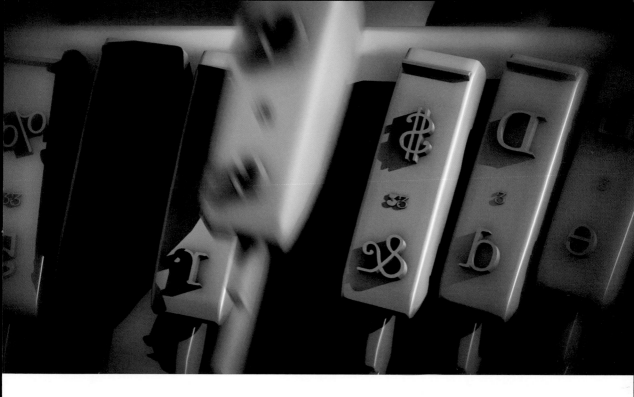

I saw the best minds of my generation
destroyed by madness . . .

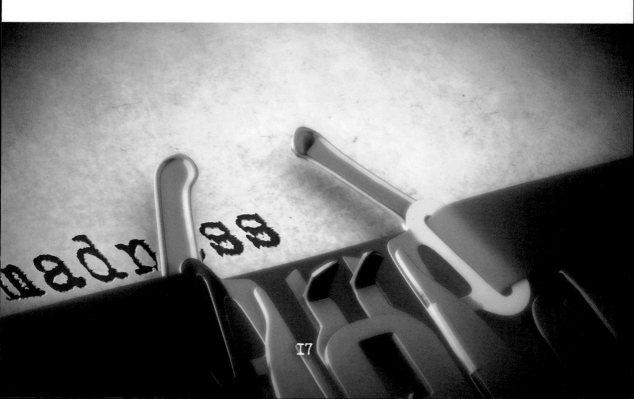

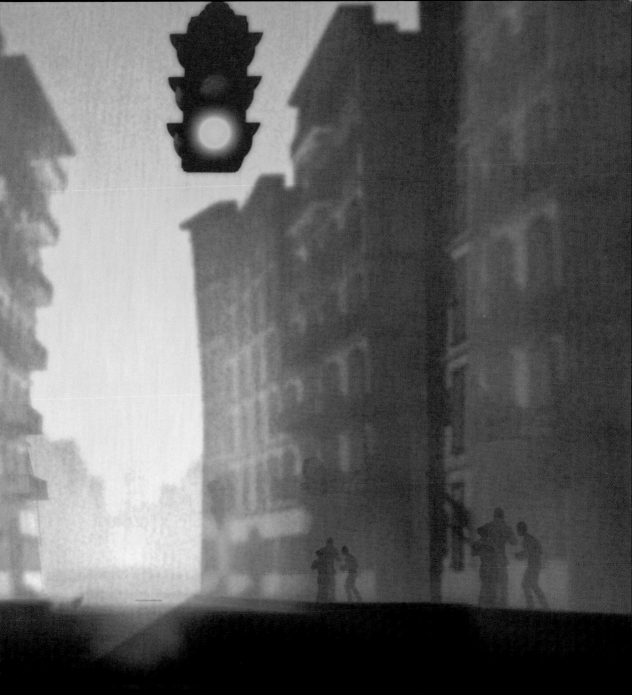

... starving hysterical naked, dragging themselves through the negro streets at dawn looking for an angry fix,

angelheaded hipsters burning for the ancient
heavenly connection to the starry dynamo in
the machinery of night,

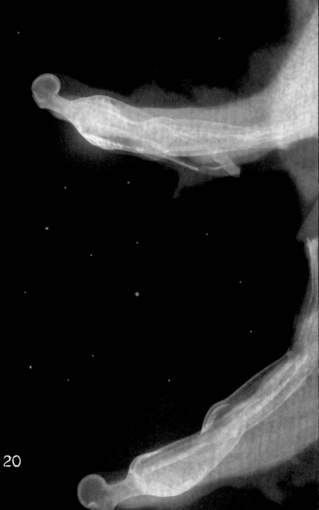

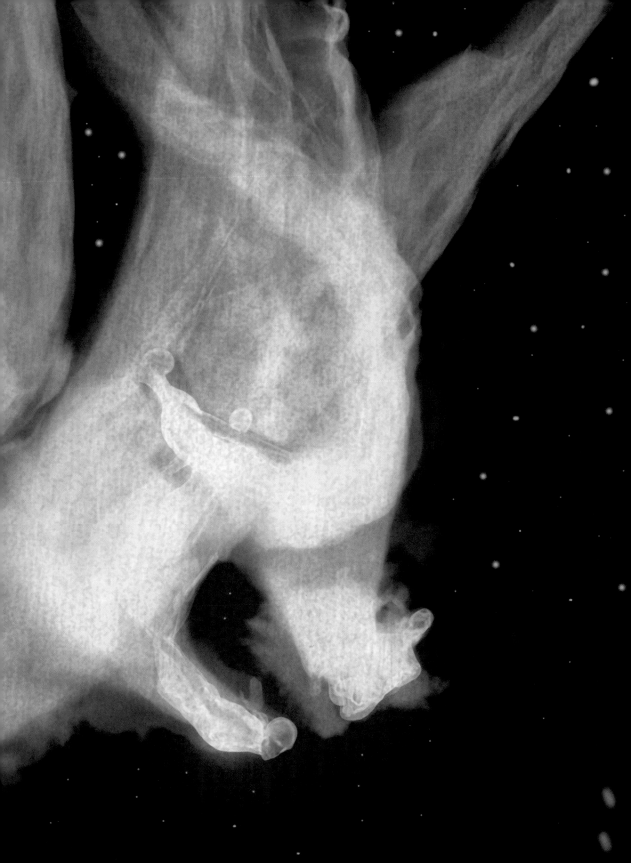

who poverty and tatters and hollow-eyed and high
    sat up smoking in the supernatural darkness
    of cold-water flats floating across the tops
    of cities contemplating jazz,

who bared their brains to Heaven under the El and
saw Mohammedan angels staggering on tenement
roofs illuminated,

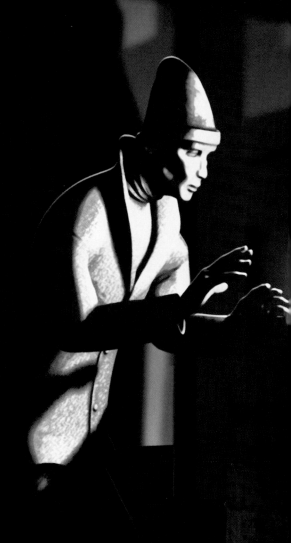

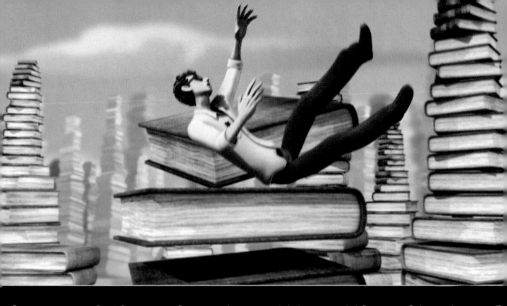

who passed **through** universities with radiant cool eyes hallucinating Arkansas and Blake-light tragedy among the scholars of war,

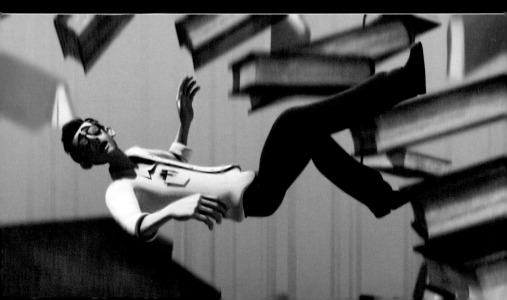

who were expelled from the academies for crazy &
publishing obscene odes on the windows of the
skull,

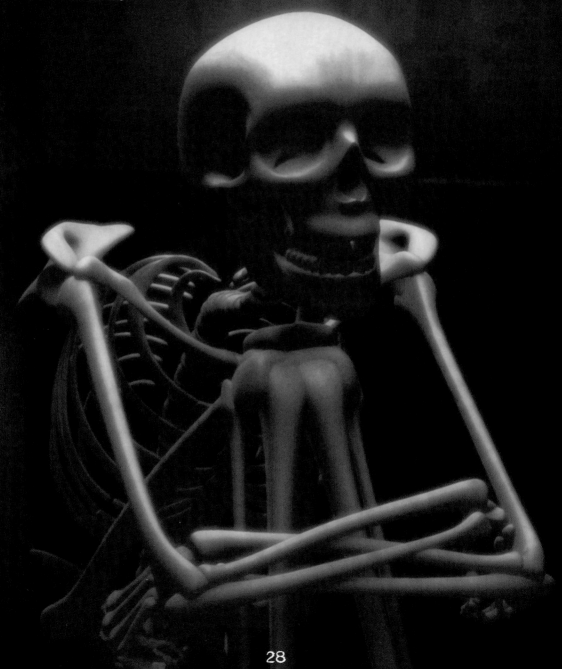

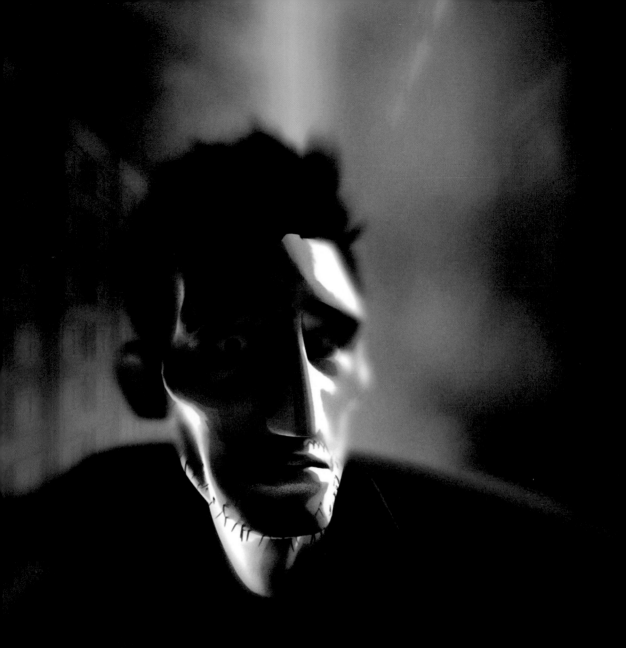

who cowered in unshaven rooms in underwear,
burning their money in wastebaskets and
listening to the Terror through the wall,

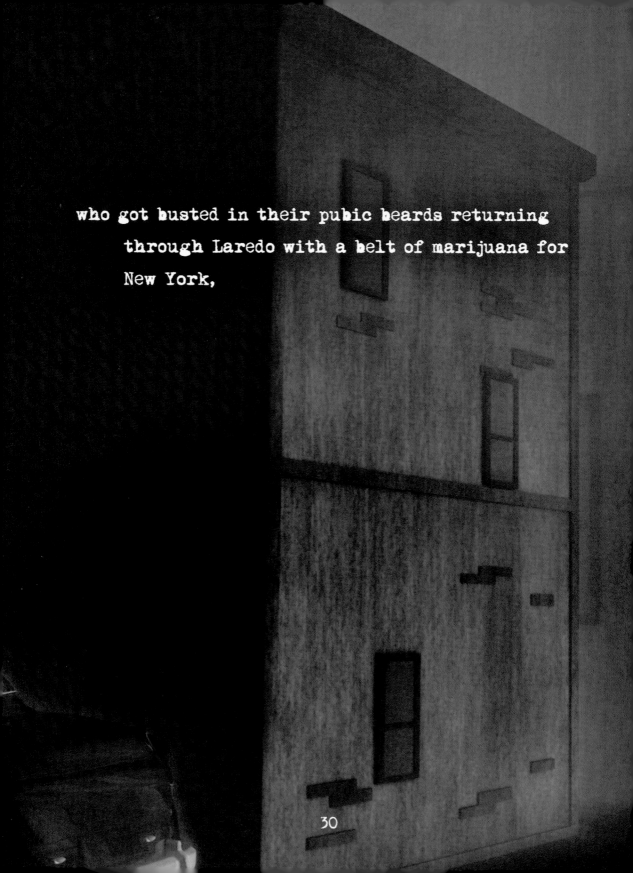

who got busted in their pubic beards returning
    through Laredo with a belt of marijuana for
New York,

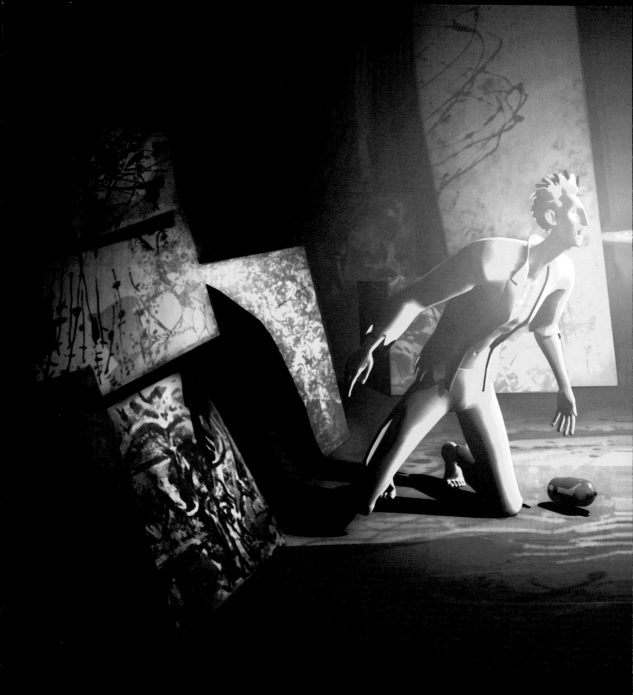

who ate fire in paint hotels or drank turpentine
in Paradise Alley, death, or purgatoried their
torsos night after night

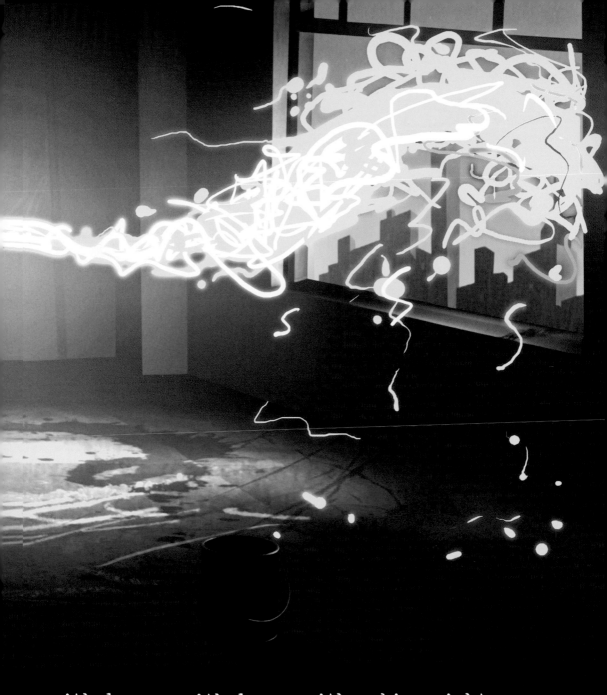

with dreams, with drugs, with waking nightmares,
alcohol and cock and endless balls,

incomparable blind streets of shuddering cloud
and lightning in the mind leaping toward
poles of Canada & Paterson, illuminating all
the motionless world of Time between,

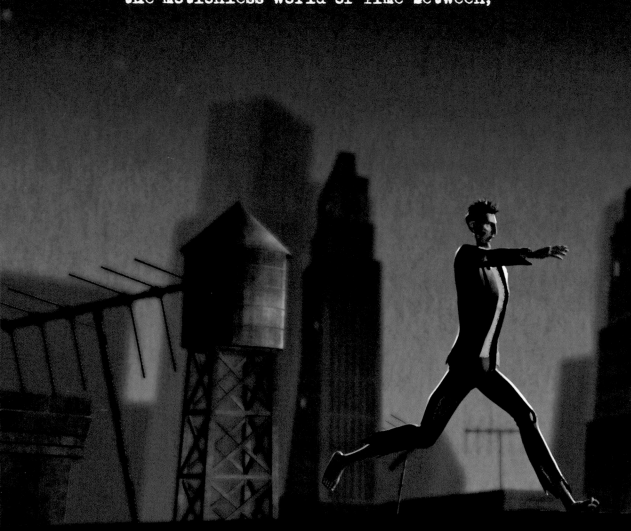

peyote solidities of halls, backyard green tree
cemetery dawns, wine drunkenness over the
rooftops, storefront boroughs of teahead
joyride neon blinking traffic light, sun and
moon and tree vibrations in the roaring
winter dusks of Brooklyn, ashcan rantings
and kind king light of mind,

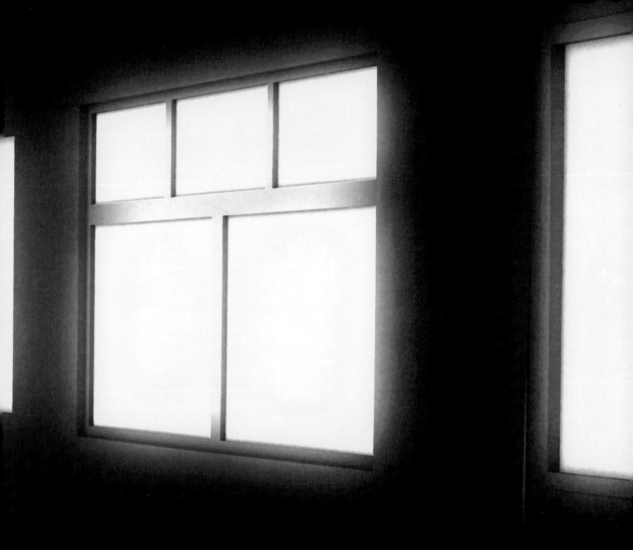

who chained themselves to subways for the endless
    ride from Battery to holy Bronx on benzedrine
    until the noise of wheels and children
    brought them down shuddering mouth-wracked
    and battered bleak of brain all drained of
    brilliance in the drear light of Zoo,

who sank all night in submarine light of
Bickford's floated out and sat through the
stale beer after noon in desolate Fugazzi's,
listening to the crack of doom on the
hydrogen jukebox,

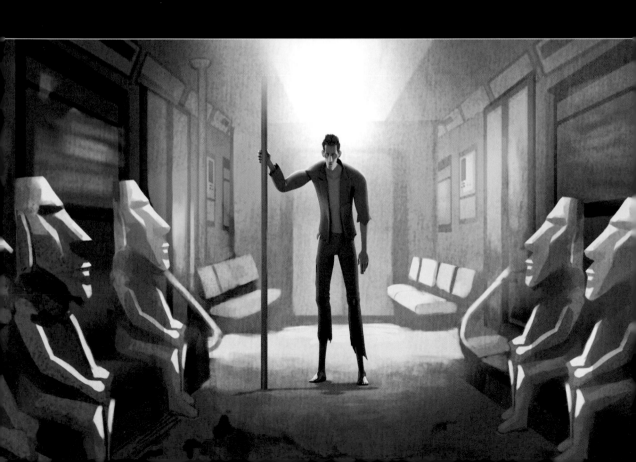

who talked continuously seventy hours from park
    to pad to bar to Bellevue to museum to the
    Brooklyn Bridge,
a lost battalion of platonic conversationalists
    jumping down the stoops off fire escapes off
    windowsills off Empire State out of the moon,
yacketayakking screaming vomiting whispering
    facts and memories and anecdotes and eyeball
    kicks and shocks of hospitals and jails and
    wars,

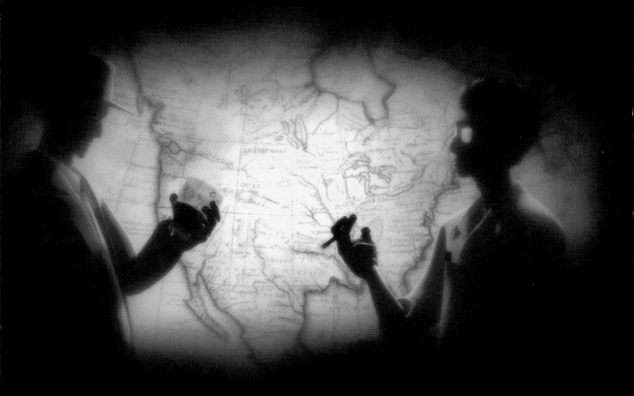

whole intellects disgorged in total recall for
seven days and nights with brilliant eyes,
meat for the Synagogue cast on the pavement,

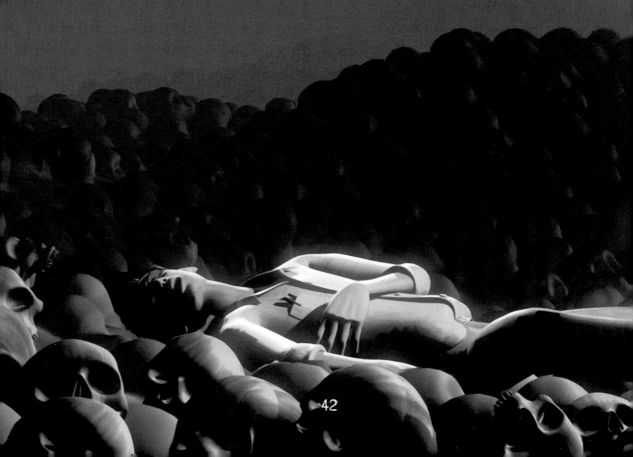

who vanished into nowhere Zen New Jersey leaving
        a trail of ambiguous picture postcards of
        Atlantic City Hall,
suffering Eastern sweats and Tangerian
        bonegrindings and migraines of China under
        junkwithdrawal in Newark's bleak furnished
        room,

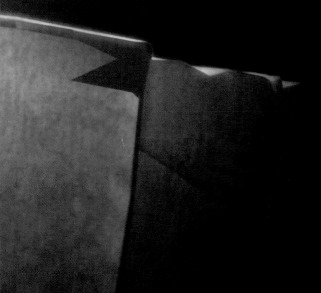

who wandered around and around at midnight in the
railroad yard wondering where to go, and went,
leaving no broken hearts,

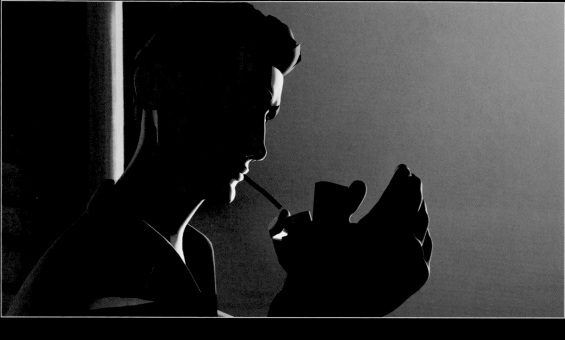

who lit cigarettes in boxcars boxcars boxcars
    racketing through snow toward lonesome farms
    in grandfather night,

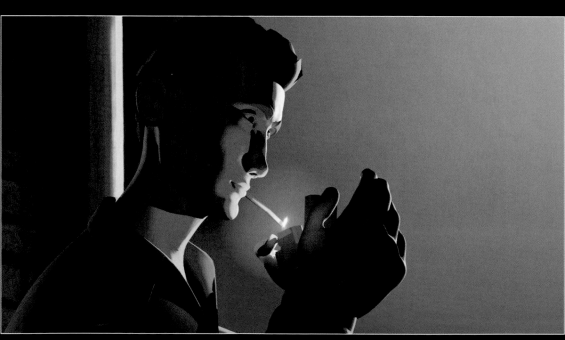

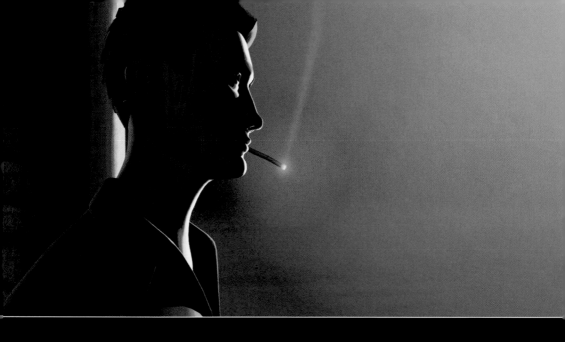

who studied Plotinus Poe St. John of the Cross
   telepathy and bop kabbalah because the cosmos
instinctively vibrated at their feet in Kansas,

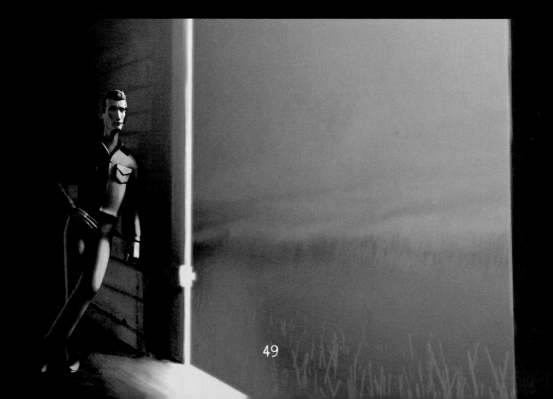

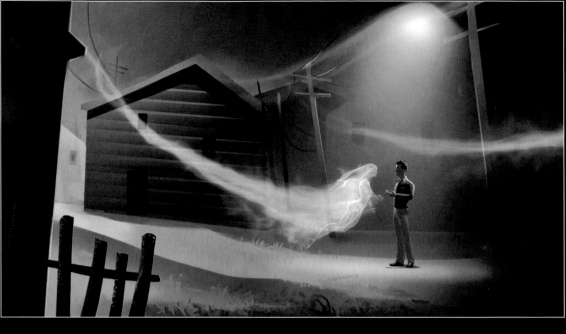

who loned it through the streets of Idaho seeking visionary indian angels who were visionary indian angels,

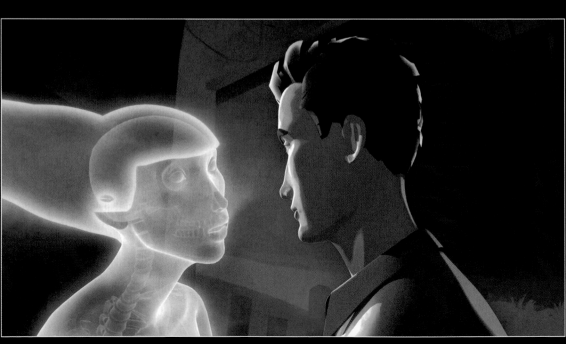

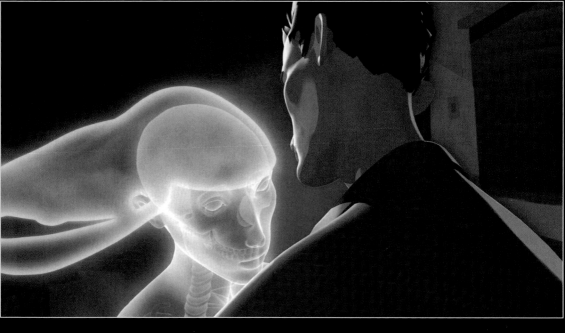

who thought they were only mad when Baltimore
gleamed in supernatural ecstasy,

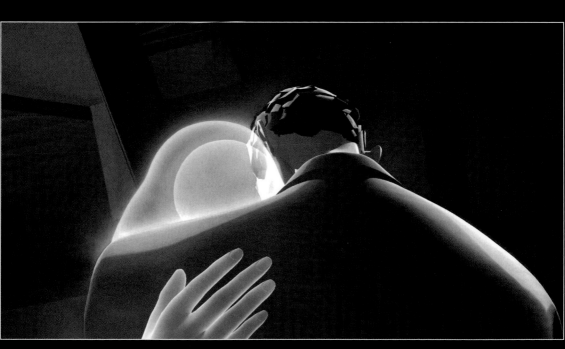

who jumped in limousines with the Chinaman of
Oklahoma on the impulse of winter midnight
street light smalltown rain,

who lounged hungry and lonesome through Houston
seeking jazz or sex or soup, and followed the
brilliant Spaniard to converse about America
and Eternity, a hopeless task, and so took ship
to Africa,

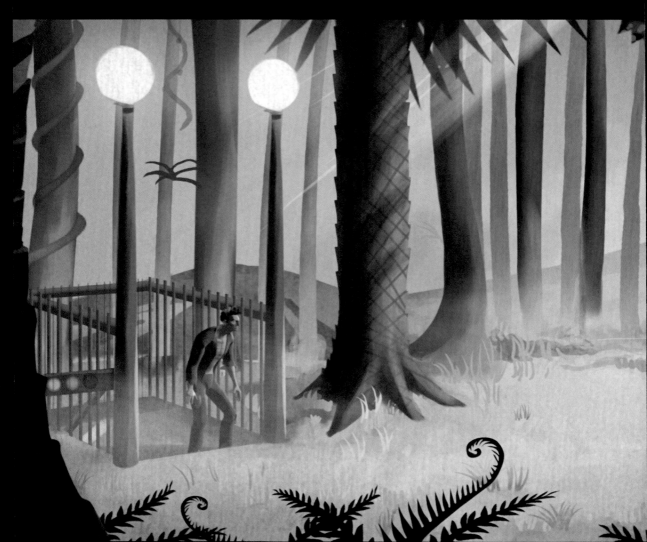

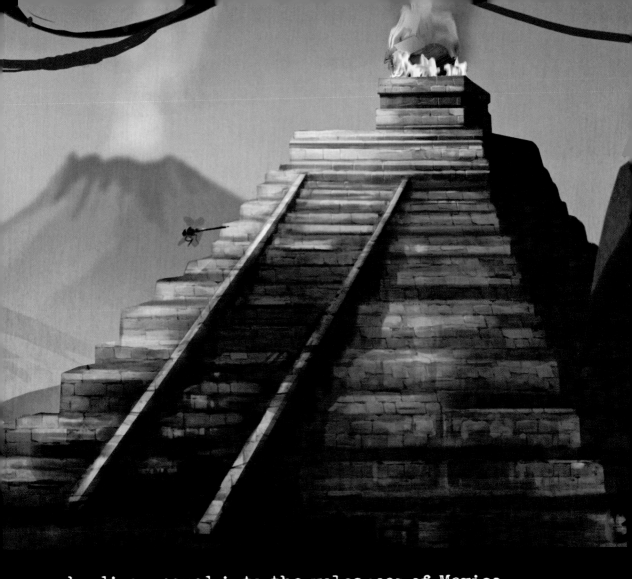

who disappeared into the volcanoes of Mexico
leaving behind nothing but the shadow of
dungarees and the lava and ash of poetry
scattered in fire place Chicago,

who reappeared on the West Coast investigating the
FBI in beards and shorts with big pacifist
eyes sexy in their dark skin passing out
incomprehensible leaflets,

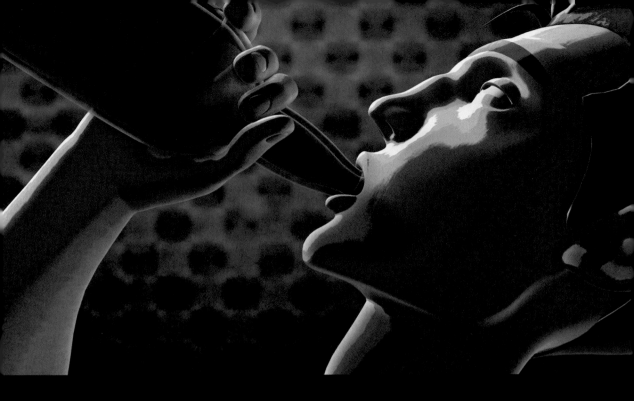

who burned cigarette holes in their arms

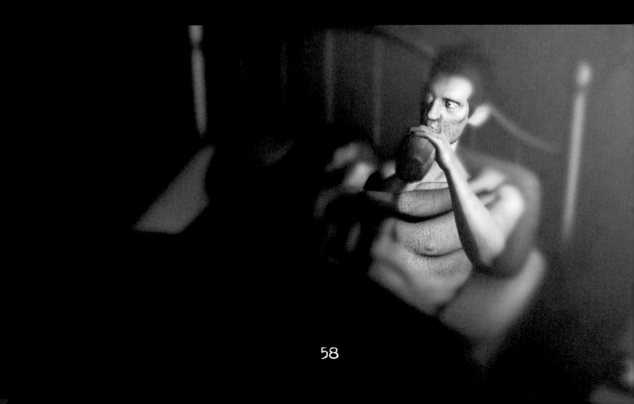

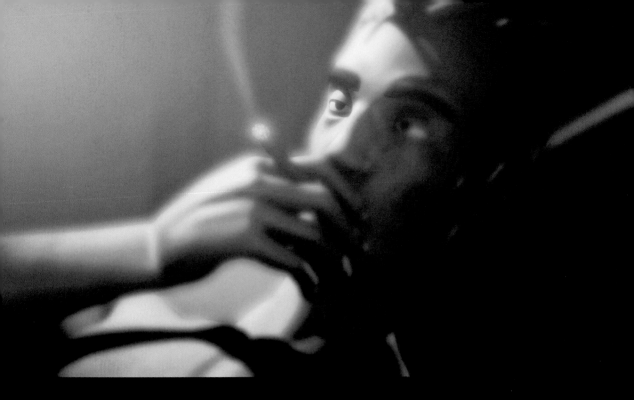

protesting the narcotic tobacco haze of
Capitalism,

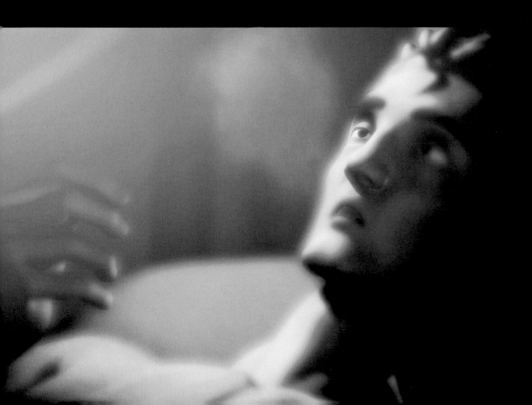

who distributed Supercommunist pamphlets in Union
    Square weeping and undressing while the
    sirens of Los Alamos wailed them down, and
    wailed down Wall, and the Staten Island ferry
    also wailed,
who broke down crying in white gymnasiums naked
    and trembling before the machinery of other
    skeletons,
who bit detectives in the neck and shrieked with
    delight in policecars for committing no crime
    but their own wild cooking pederasty and
    intoxication,

who howled on their knees in the subway and were dragged off the roof waving genitals and manuscripts,

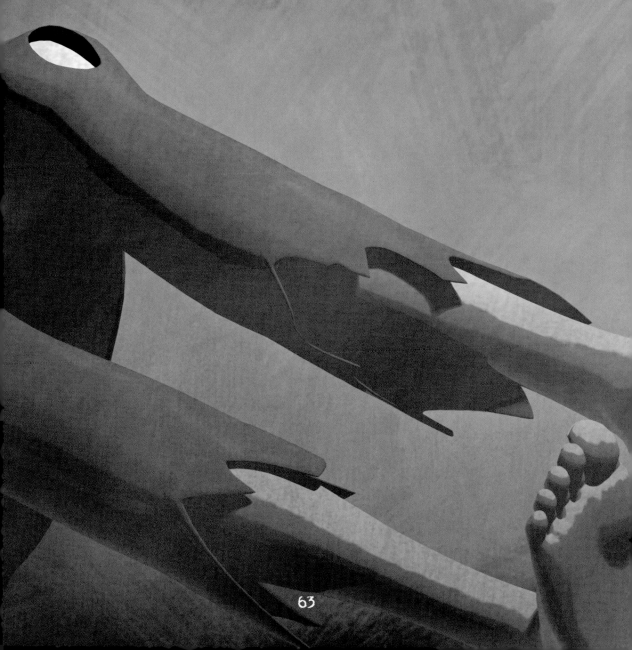

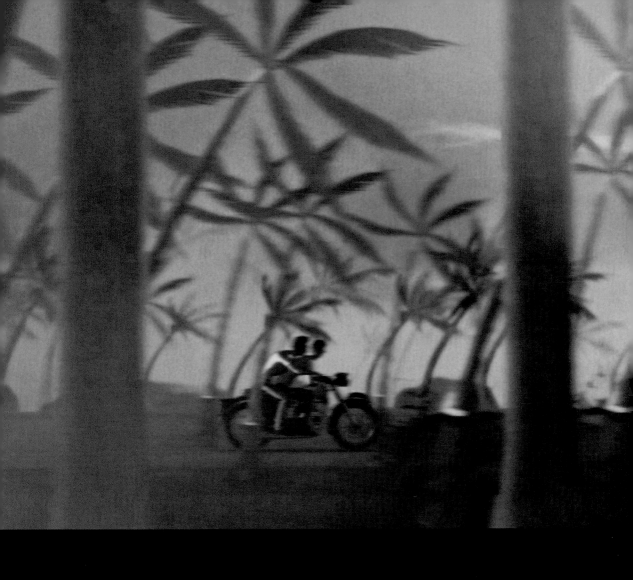

who let themselves be fucked in the ass by

saintly motorcyclists, and screamed with joy,

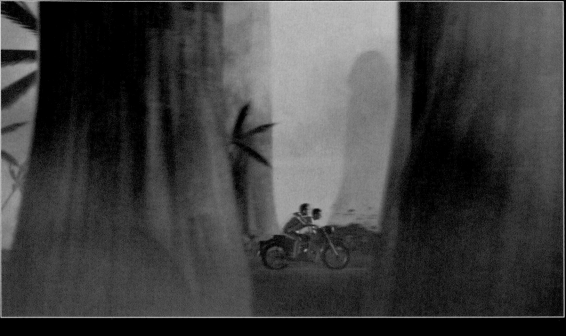

who blew and were blown by those human seraphim,

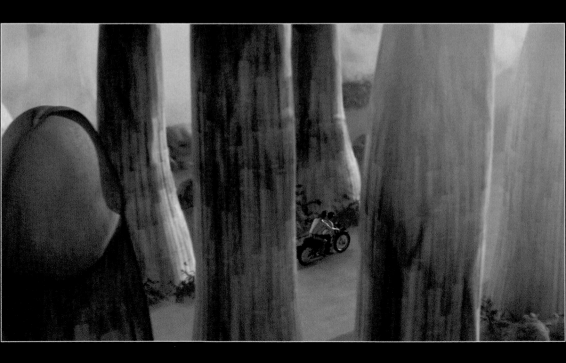

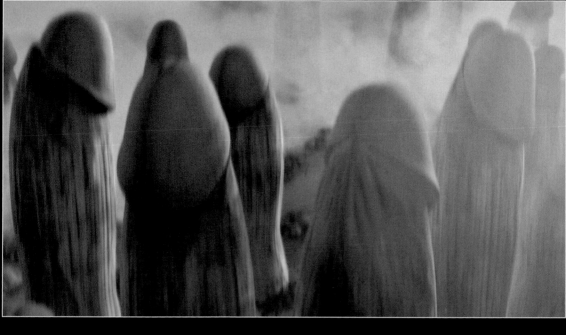

the sailors, caresses of Atlantic and
Caribbean love,

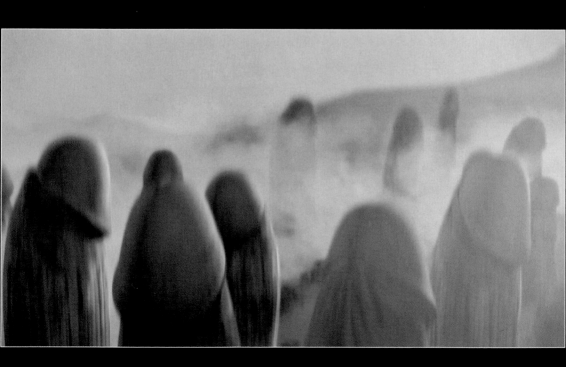

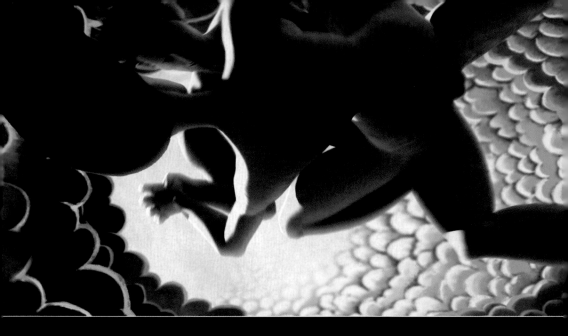

who balled in the morning in the evenings in rose-
gardens and the grass of public parks and
cemeteries scattering their semen freely to
whomever come who may,

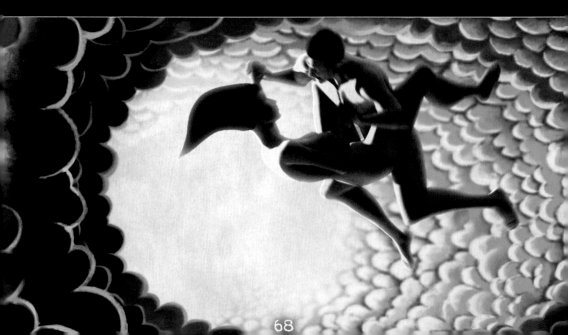

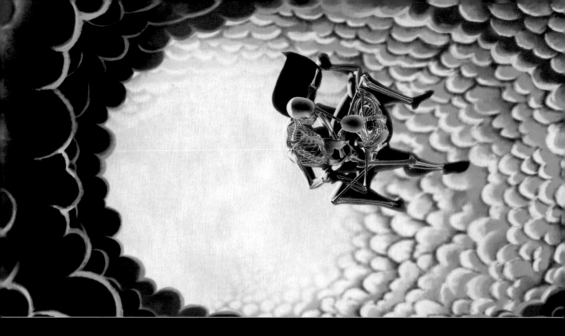

who hiccuped endlessly trying to giggle but wound up with a sob behind a partition in a Turkish Bath when the blond & naked angel came to pierce them with a sword,

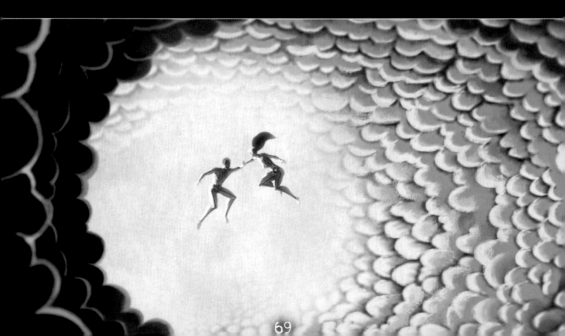

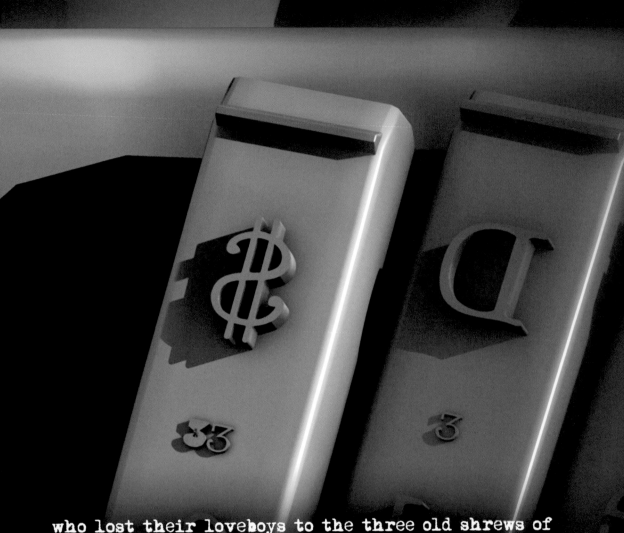

who lost their loveboys to the three old shrews of
fate the one eyed shrew of the heterosexual
dollar the one eyed shrew that winks out of
the womb and the one eyed shrew that does
nothing but sit on her ass and snip the
intellectual golden threads of the craftsman's
loom,

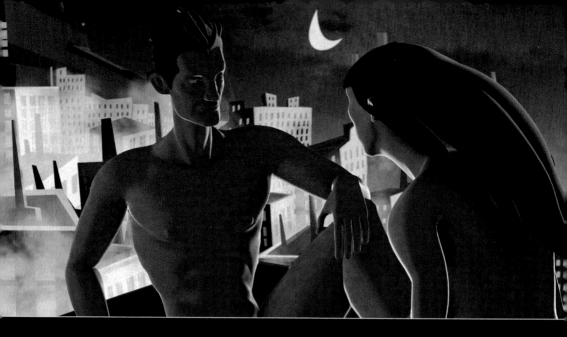

who copulated ecstatic and insatiate with a
bottle of beer a sweetheart a package of
cigarettes a candle and fell off the bed,
and continued along the floor and down the

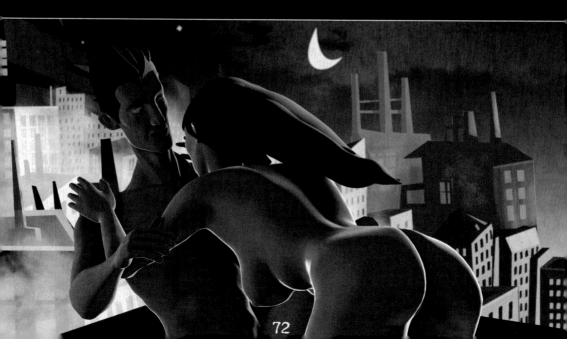

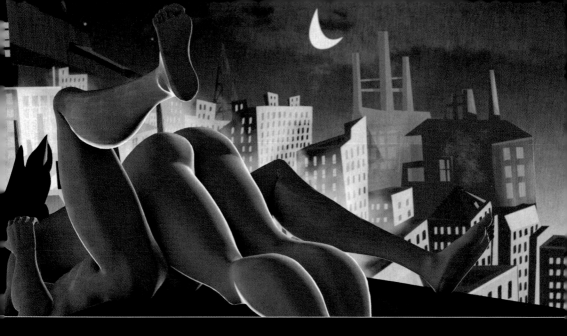

hall and ended fainting on the wall with a
vision of ultimate cunt and come eluding
the last gyzym of consciousness,

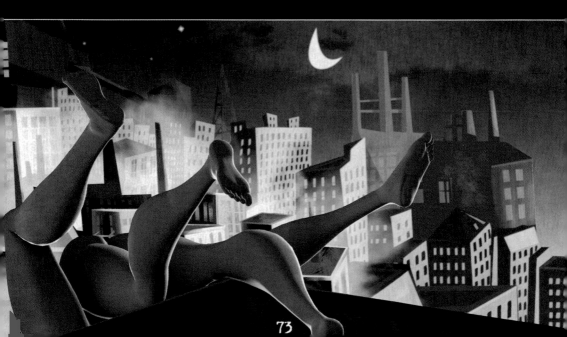

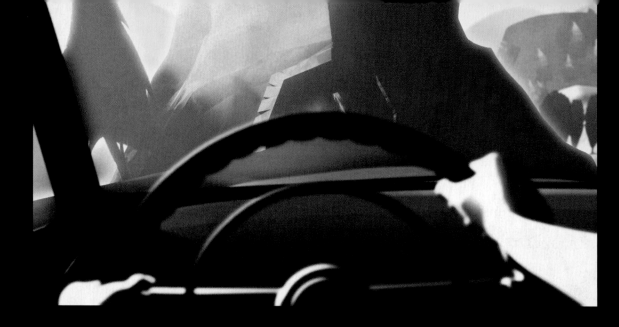

who sweetened the snatches of a million girls
trembling in the sunset, and were red eyed
in the morning but prepared to sweeten the
snatch of the sun rise, flashing buttocks
under barns and naked in the lake,

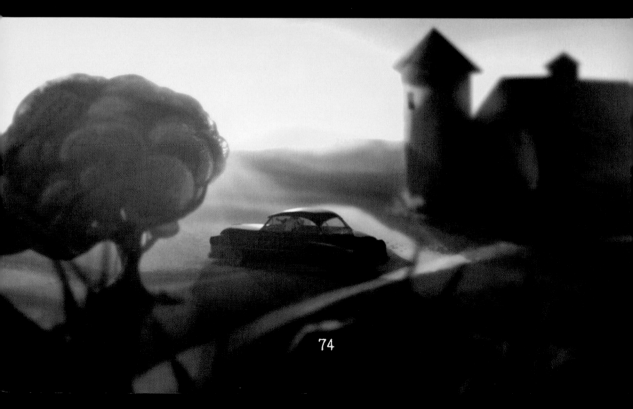

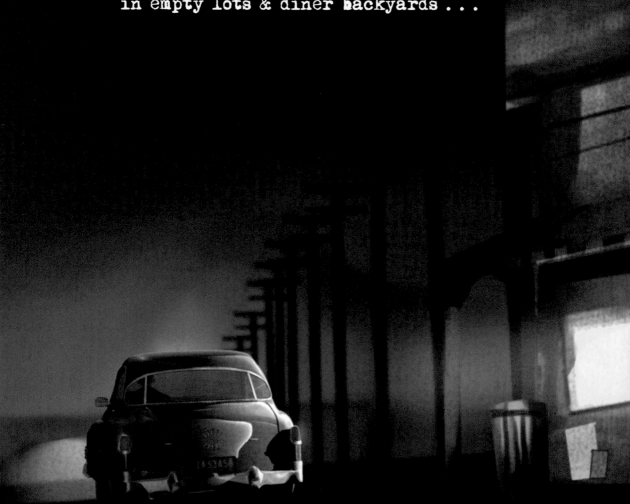

who went out whoring through Colorado in myriad
  stolen night-cars, N.C., secret hero of these
  poems, cocksman and Adonis of Denver--joy to
  the memory of his innumerable lays of girls
  in empty lots & diner backyards . . .

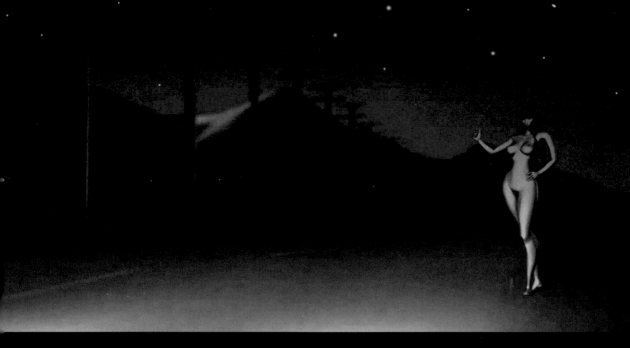

... moviehouses' rickety rows, on mountaintops
in caves or with gaunt waitresses in familiar
roadside lonely petticoat upliftings &

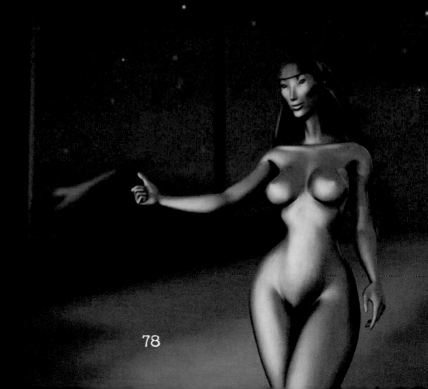

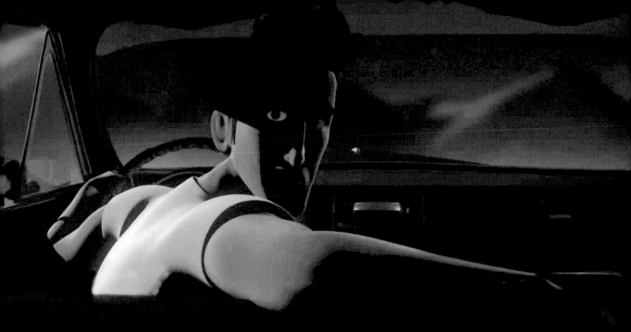

especially secret gas-station solipsisms of
johns, & hometown alleys too,

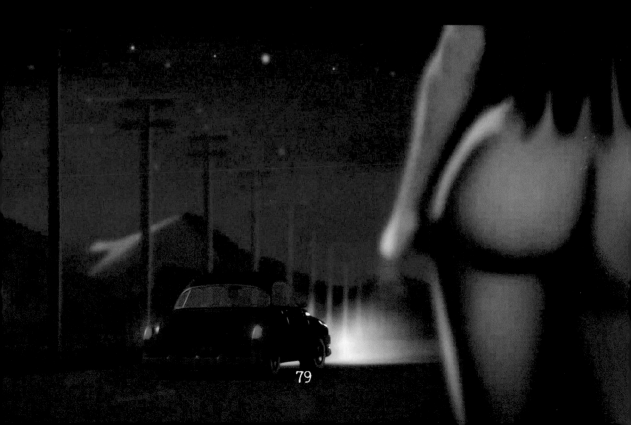

BAR
DESTROYED BY MADNESS
STARVING HYSTERICAL
NAKED XXX
ALCOHOL & COCK & ENDLESS BALLS
WHO COPULATED ECSTATIC & INSATIATE
HOTEL
CHOP SUEY
BAR

who faded out in vast sordid movies, were shifted
in dreams, woke on a sudden Manhattan, and
picked themselves up out of basements hung
over with heartless Tokay and horrors of
Third Avenue iron dreams & stumbled to
unemployment offices,

BAR
DESTROYED BY MADNESS
STARVING HYSTERICAL
NAKED XXX
HOTEL
CHOP SUEY
THE TONGUE &
& HAND & ASS
HOLY! HOLY!
BAR

BAR
DESTROYED BY MADNESS
STARVING HYSTERICAL
NAKED XXX
HOTEL
CHOP SUEY
THE TONGUE &
& HAND & ASS
HOLY! HOLY!
BAR

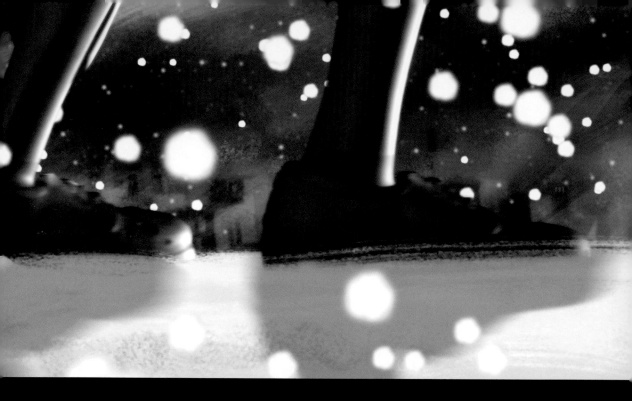

who walked all night with their shoes full of
blood on the snowbank docks waiting for a

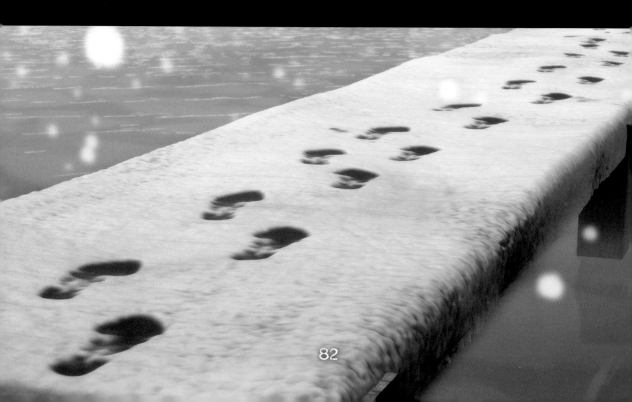

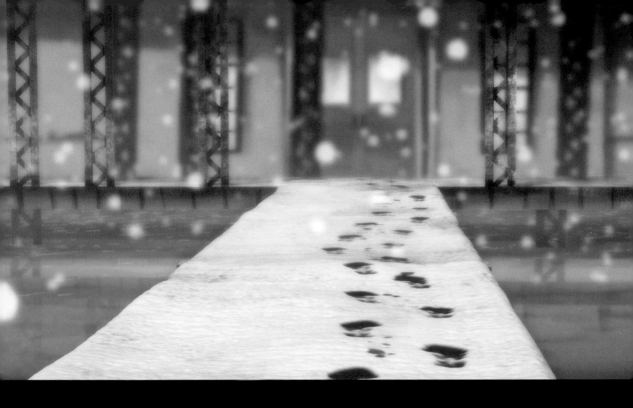

door in the East River to open to a room full
of steam-heat and opium,

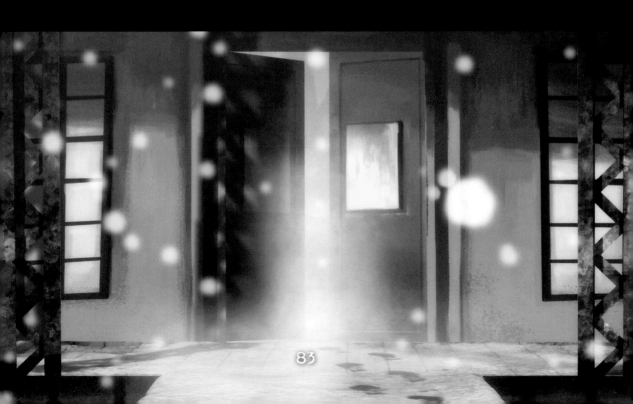

who created great suicidal dramas on the
    apartment cliff-banks of the Hudson under
    the wartime blue floodlight of the moon &
    their heads shall be crowned with laurel in
    oblivion,

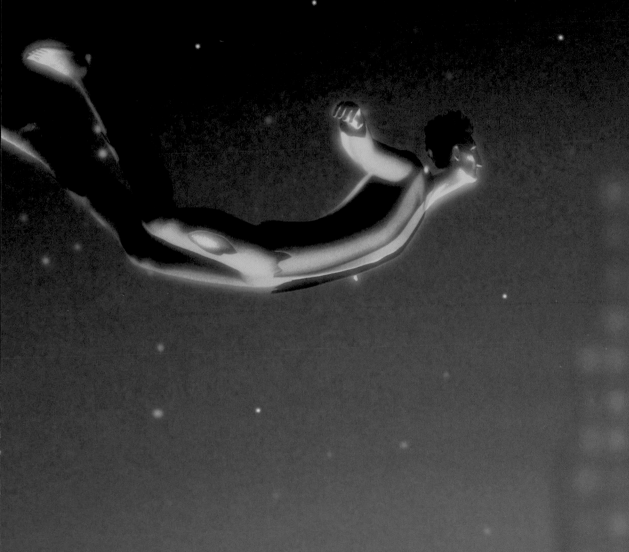

who ate the lamb stew of the imagination or
   digested the crab at the muddy bottom of the
   rivers of Bowery,
who wept at the romance of the streets with their
   pushcarts full of onions and bad music,

who sat in boxes breathing in the darkness under
the bridge, and rose up to build harpsichords
in their lofts,

who coughed on the sixth floor of Harlem crowned
with flame under the tubercular sky
surrounded by orange crates of theology,

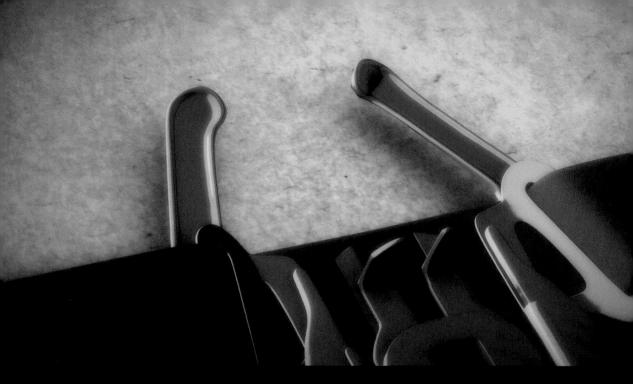

who scribbled all night rocking and rolling over
lofty incantations which in the yellow
morning were stanzas of gibberish,

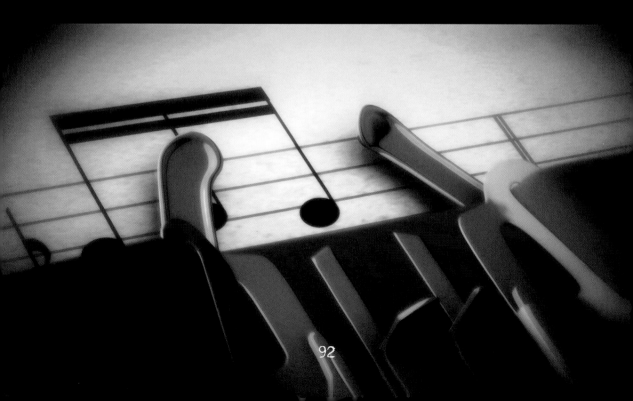

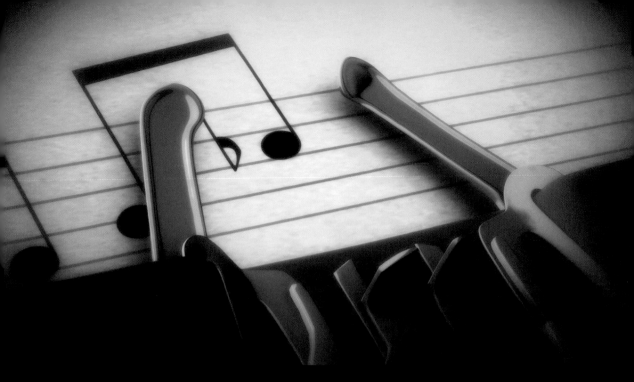

who cooked rotten animals lung heart feet tail
borsht & tortillas dreaming of the pure
vegetable kingdom,

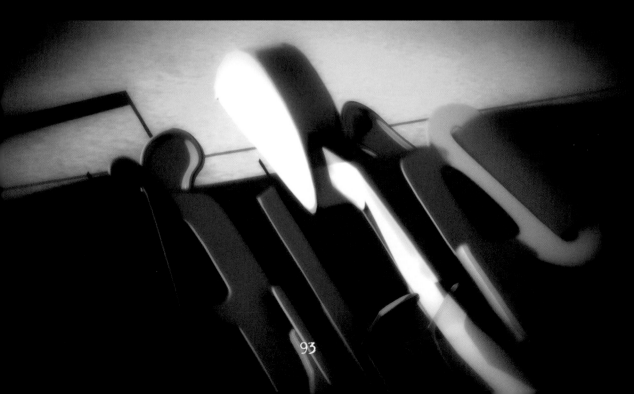

who plunged themselves under meat trucks looking
    for an egg,
who threw their watches off the roof to cast their
    ballot for Eternity outside of Time, & alarm
    clocks fell on their heads every day for the
    next decade,

who cut their wrists three times successively
    unsuccessfully, gave up and were forced to
    open antique stores where they thought they
    were growing old and cried,

who were burned alive in their innocent flannel
suits on Madison Avenue amid blasts of leaden
verse & the tanked-up clatter of the iron
regiments of fashion & the nitroglycerine
shrieks of the fairies of advertising . . .

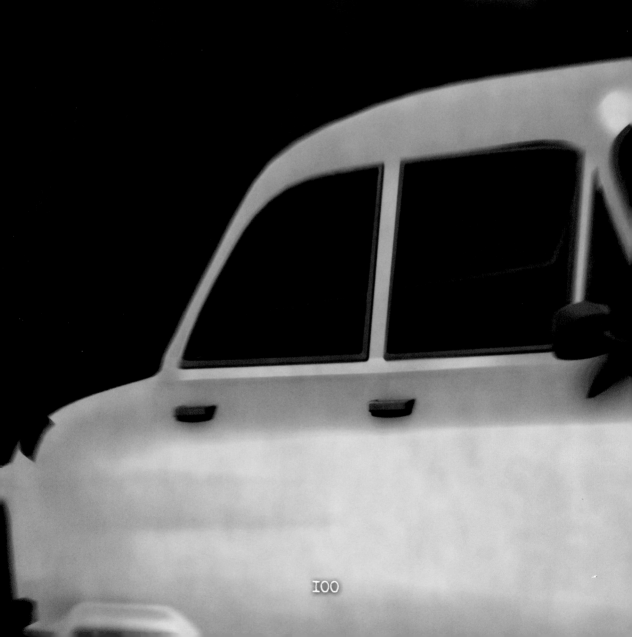

. . . & the mustard gas of sinister intelligent editors, or were run down by the drunken taxicabs of Absolute Reality,

who jumped off the Brooklyn Bridge this actually
    happened and walked away unknown and
    forgotten into the ghostly daze of Chinatown
    soup alleyways & firetrucks, not even one
    free beer,

who sang out of their windows in despair, fell out
of the subway window, jumped in the filthy
Passaic, leaped on negroes, cried all over the
street, danced on broken wineglasses barefoot
smashed phonograph records of nostalgic
European 1930s German jazz finished the
whiskey and threw up groaning into the bloody
toilet, moans in their ears and the blast of
colossal steam whistles,

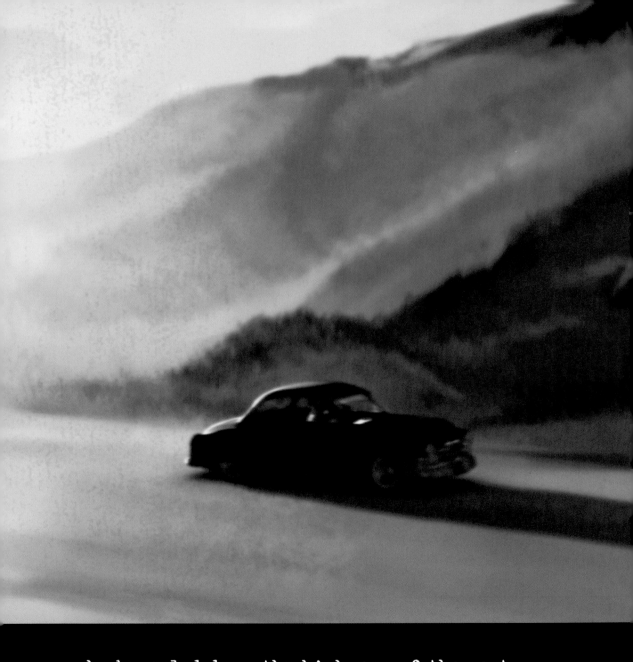

who barreled down the highways of the past
journeying to each other's hotrod-Golgotha
jail-solitude watch or Birmingham jazz

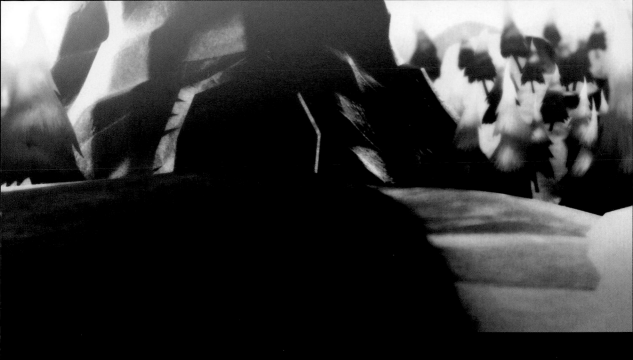

who drove crosscountry seventytwo hours to find
out if I had a vision or you had a vision or
he had a vision to find out Eternity,

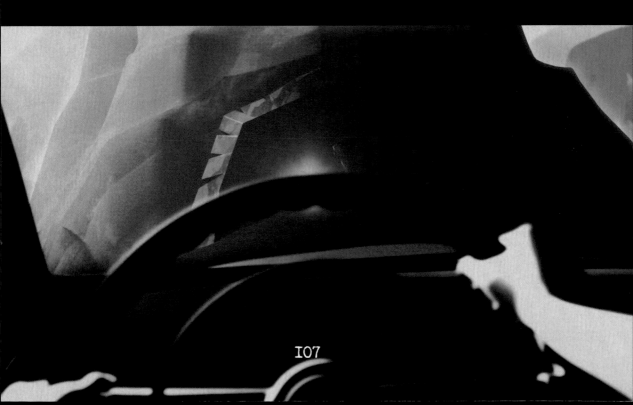

who journeyed to Denver, who died in Denver, who
came back to Denver & waited in vain, who
watched over Denver & brooded & loned in
Denver and finally went away to find out the
Time, & now Denver is lonesome for her heroes,

who fell on their knees in hopeless cathedrals
praying for each other's salvation and light

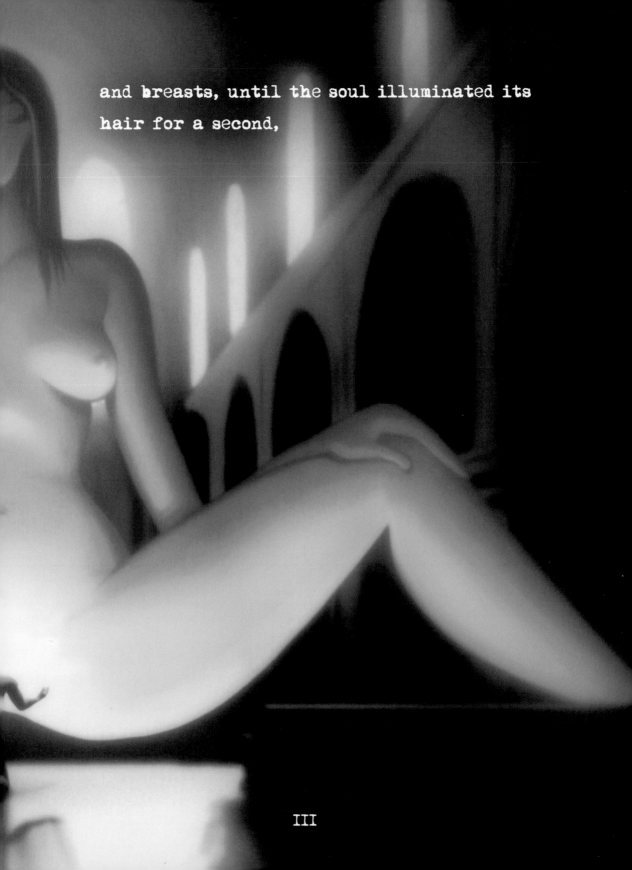

and breasts, until the soul illuminated its
hair for a second,

III

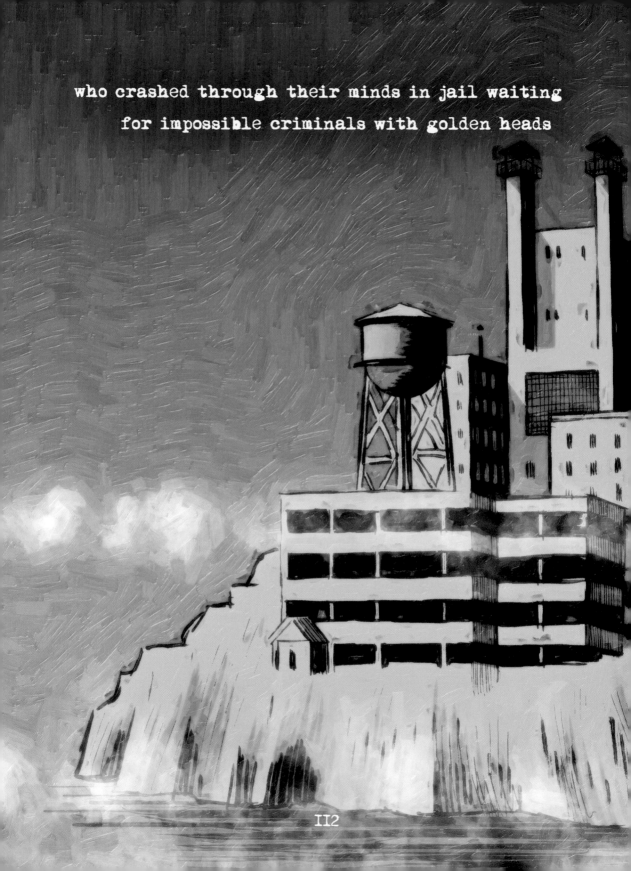

who crashed through their minds in jail waiting
for impossible criminals with golden heads

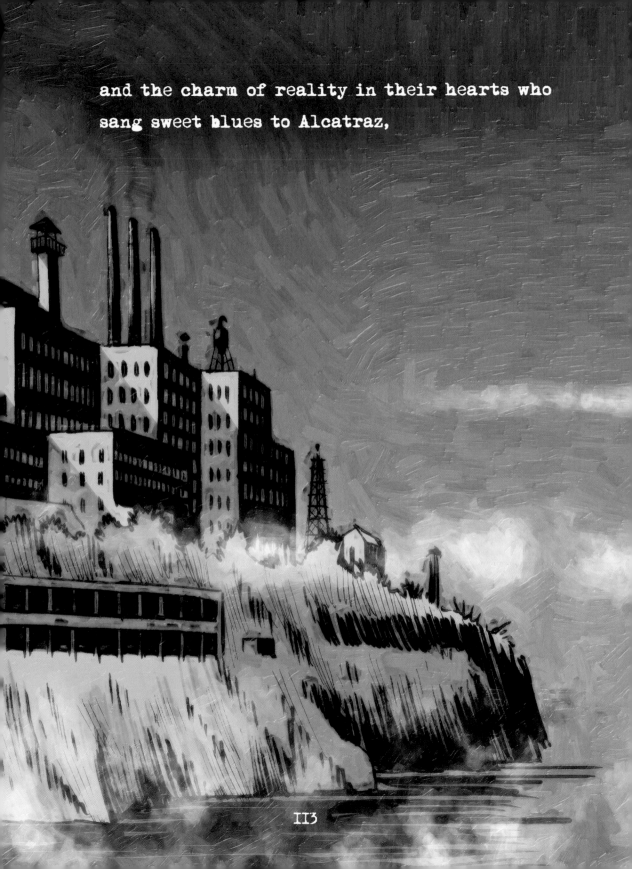

and the charm of reality in their hearts who
sang sweet blues to Alcatraz,

who retired to Mexico to cultivate a habit, or
        Rocky Mount to tender Buddha or Tangiers to
        boys or Southern Pacific to the black
        locomotive or Harvard to Narcissus to Woodlawn
        to the daisychain or grave,

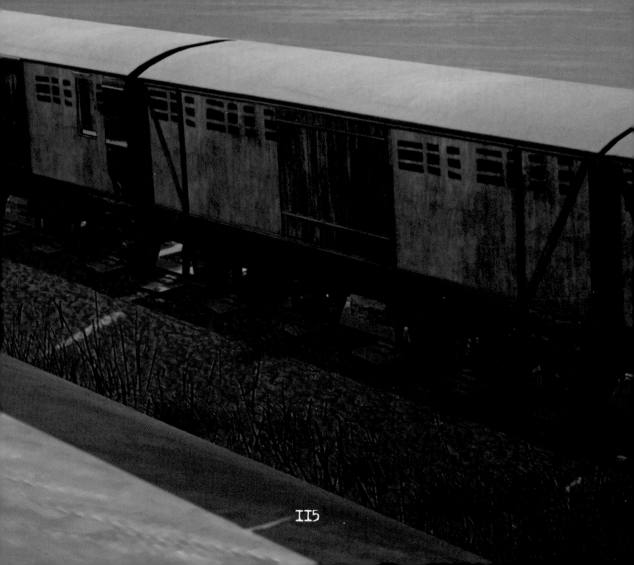

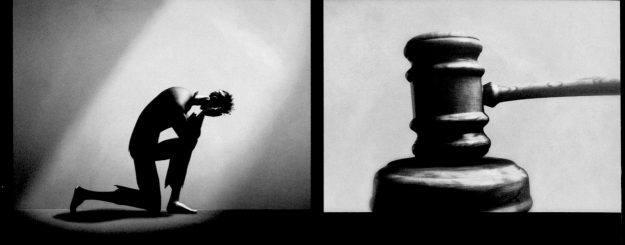

who demanded sanity trials accusing the radio of
hypnotism & were left with their insanity &
their hands & a hung jury,

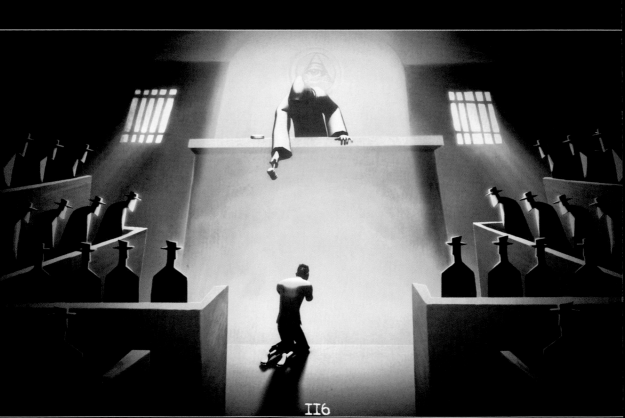

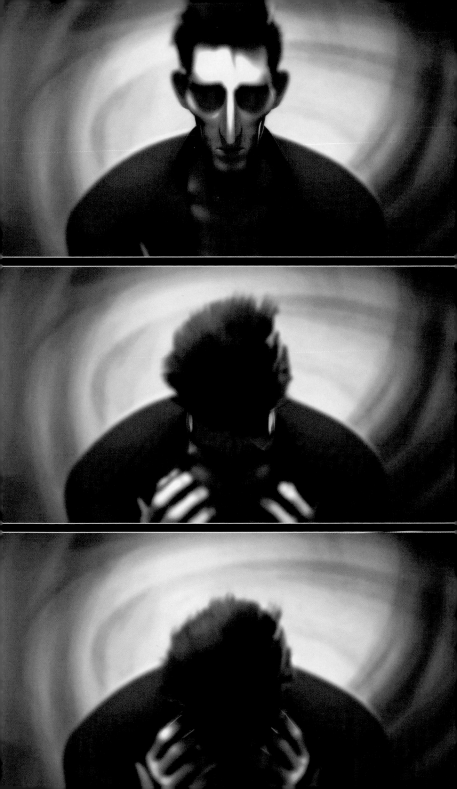

who threw potato salad at CCNY lecturers on

    Dadaism and subsequently presented themselves

    on the granite steps of the madhouse with

    shaven heads and harlequin speech of suicide,

    demanding instantaneous lobotomy,

and who were given instead the concrete void of
insulin Metrazol electricity hydrotherapy
psychotherapy occupational therapy pingpong
& amnesia,

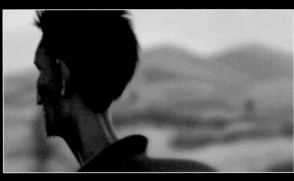

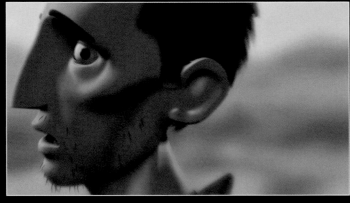

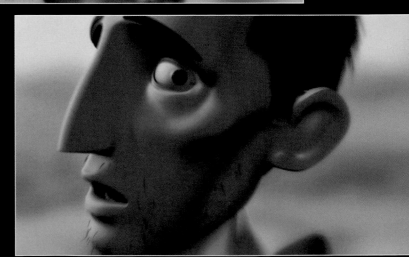

who in humorless protest overturned only one
symbolic pingpong table, resting briefly in
catatonia,

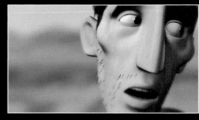

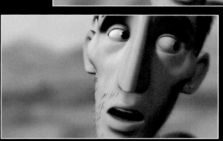

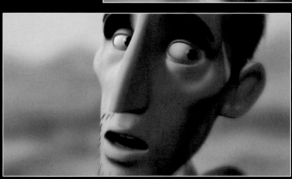

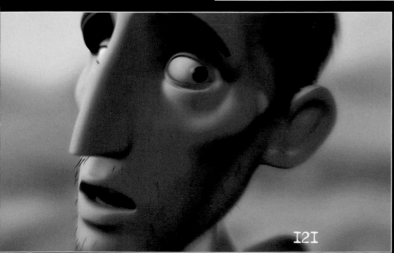

returning years later truly bald except for a wig
    of blood, and tears and fingers, to the visible
    mad man doom of the wards of the madtowns of
    the East,
Pilgrim State's Rockland's and Greystone's foetid
    halls, bickering with the echoes of the soul,
    rocking and rolling in the midnight solitude-
    bench dolmen-realms of love, dream of life a
    nightmare, bodies turned to stone as heavy as
    the moon,

with mother finally ******, and the last fantastic
book flung out of the tenement window, and
the last door closed at 4. A.M. and the last
telephone slammed at the wall in reply and
the last furnished room emptied down to the
last piece of mental furniture, a yellow paper
rose twisted on a wire hanger in the closet,
and even that imaginary, nothing but a
hopeful little bit of hallucination--

ah, carl, while you are not safe I am not safe, and
now you're really in the total animal soup of
time--

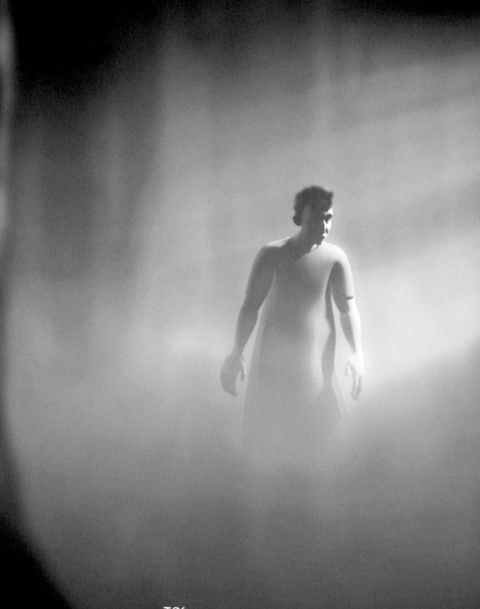

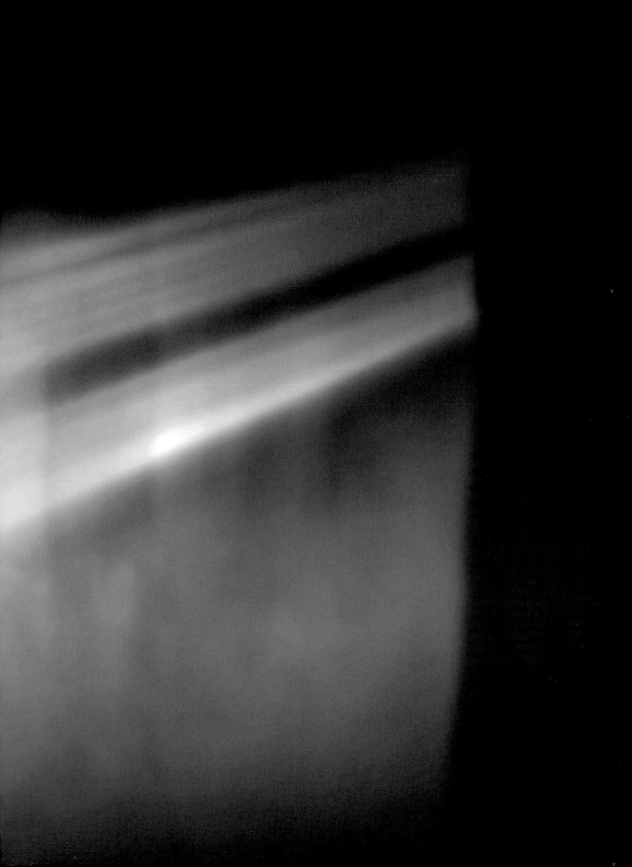

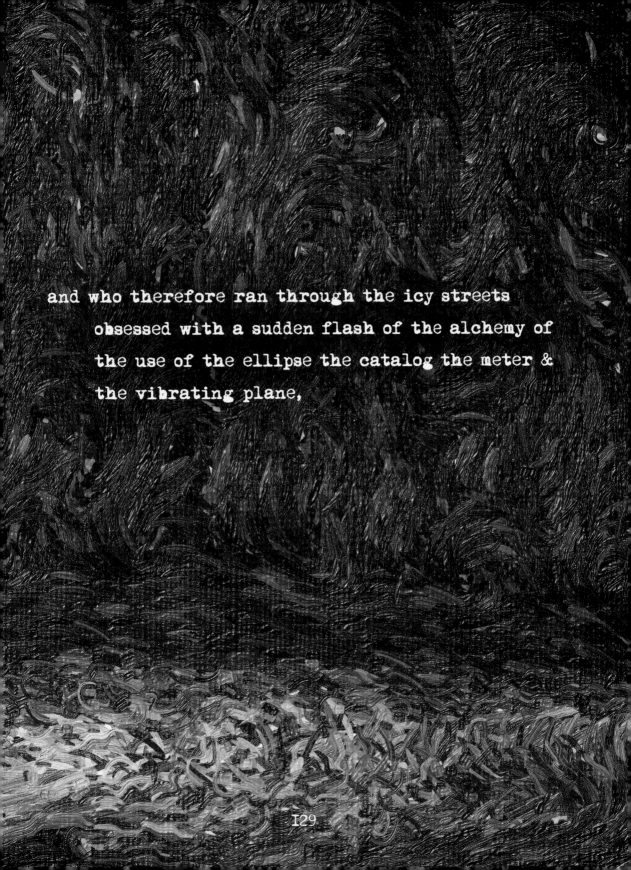

and who therefore ran through the icy streets
    obsessed with a sudden flash of the alchemy of
    the use of the ellipse the catalog the meter &
    the vibrating plane,

who dreamt and made incarnate gaps in Time & Space
   through images juxtaposed, and trapped the
   archangel of the soul between 2 visual images
   and joined the elemental verbs and set the
   noun and dash of consciousness together
   jumping with sensation of Pater Omnipotens
   Aeterna Deus

R
F
G
V

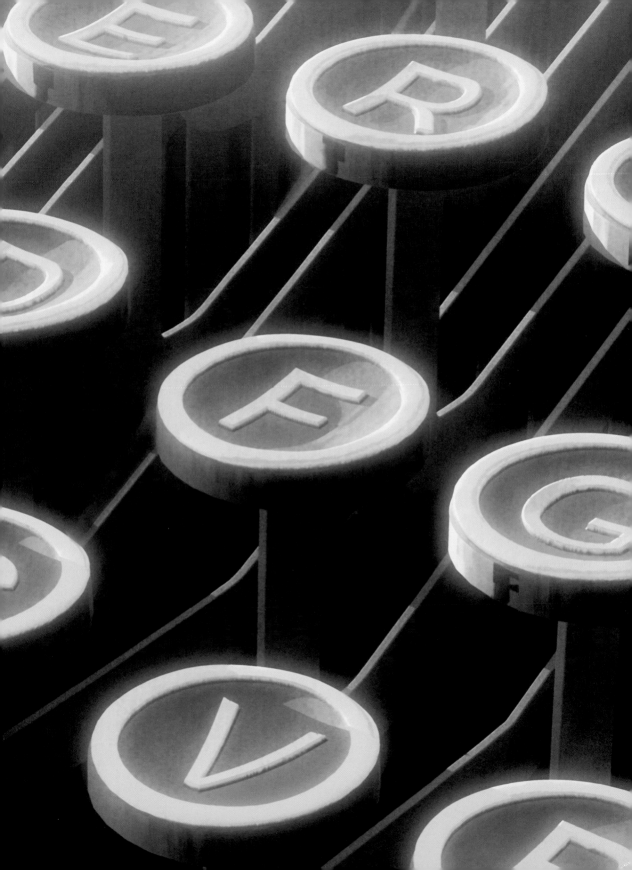

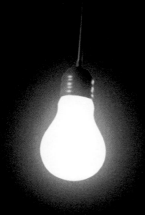

to recreate the syntax and measure of poor human
  prose and stand before you speechless and
  intelligent and shaking with shame, rejected
  yet confessing out the soul to conform to the
  rhythm of thought in his naked and endless
  head,

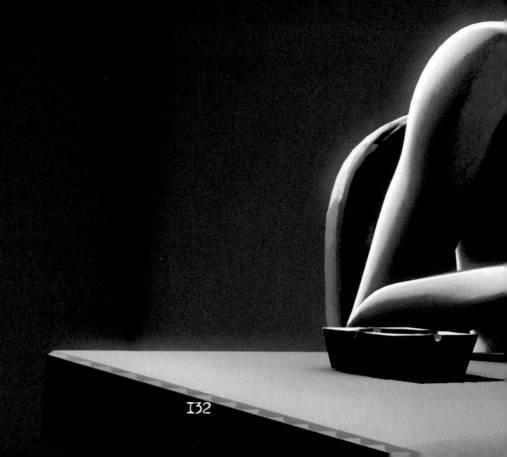

the madman bum and angel beat in Time, unknown,
yet putting down here what might be left to
say in time come after death,

and rose reincarnate in the ghostly clothes of jazz
in the goldhorn shadow of the band and blew
the suffering of America's naked mind for love
into an eli eli lamma lamma sabacthani
saxophone cry that shivered the cities down
to the last radio

with the absolute heart of the poem of life
    butchered out of their own bodies good to eat
    a thousand years.

II

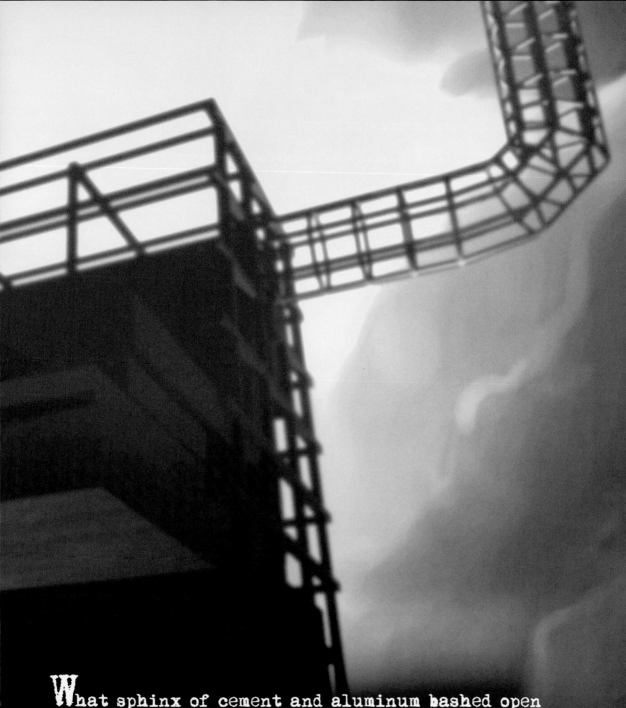

What sphinx of cement and aluminum bashed open
their skulls and ate up their brains and
imagination?

Moloch! Solitude! Filth! Ugliness! Ashcans and
unobtainable dollars! Children screaming
under the stairways! Boys sobbing in armies!
Old men weeping in the parks!
Moloch! Moloch! Nightmare of Moloch! Moloch the
loveless! Mental Moloch! Moloch the heavy
judger of men!

Moloch the incomprehensible prison! Moloch the
crossbone soulless jailhouse and Congress of
sorrows! Moloch whose buildings are judgment!
Moloch the vast stone of war! Moloch the
stunned governments!

Moloch whose mind is pure machinery! Moloch whose blood is running money! Moloch whose fingers are ten armies! Moloch whose breast is a cannibal dynamo! Moloch whose ear is a smoking tomb!

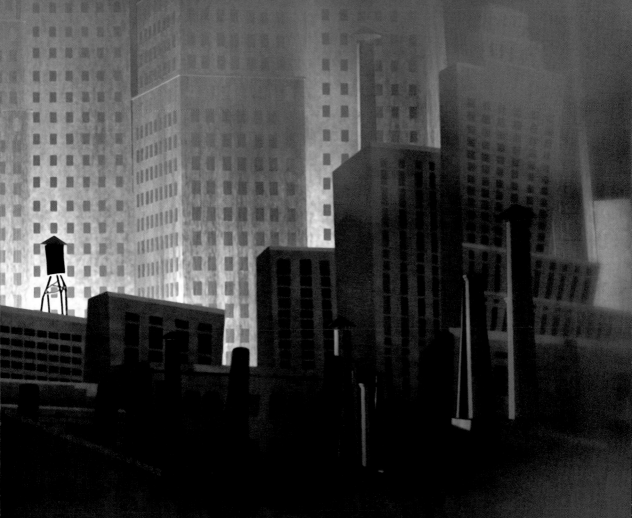

Moloch whose eyes are a thousand blind windows!
Moloch whose skyscrapers stand in the long
streets like endless Jehovahs! Moloch whose
factories dream and croak in the fog! Moloch
whose smokestacks and antennae crown the
cities!

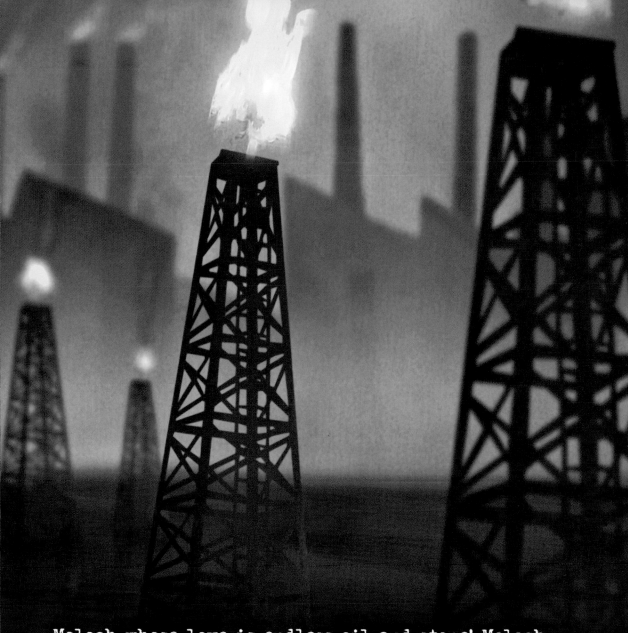

Moloch whose love is endless oil and stone! Moloch
whose soul is electricity and banks! Moloch
whose poverty is the specter of genius! Moloch
whose fate is a cloud of sexless hydrogen!
Moloch whose name is the Mind!

Moloch in whom I sit lonely! Moloch in whom I dream
    Angels! Crazy in Moloch! Cocksucker in Moloch!
    Lacklove and manless in Moloch!
Moloch who entered my soul early! Moloch in whom I
    am a consciousness without a body! Moloch who
    frightened me out of my natural ecstasy!
    Moloch whom I abandon! Wake up in Moloch!
    Light streaming out of the sky!

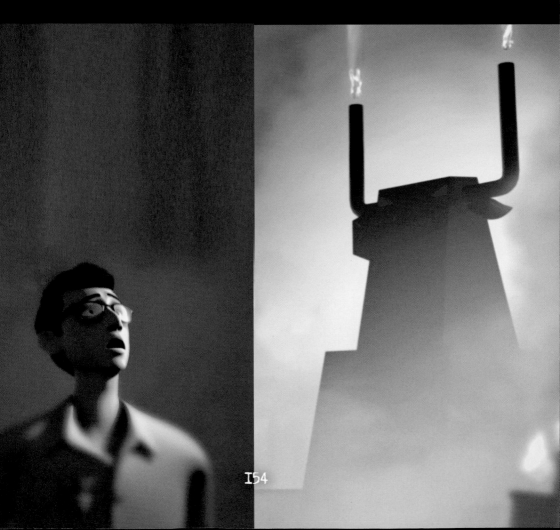

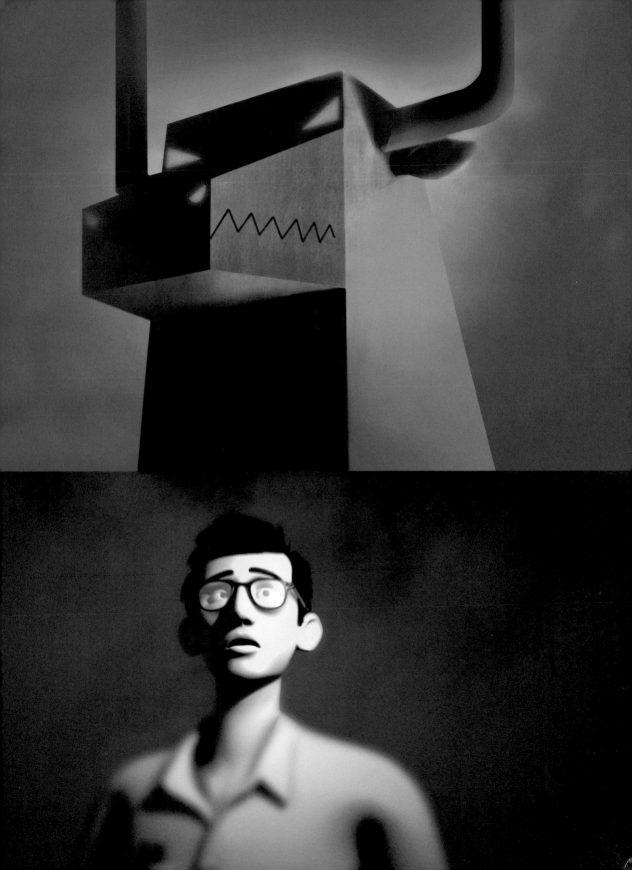

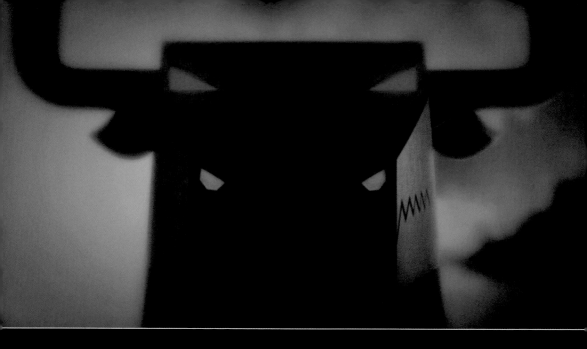

Moloch! Moloch! Robot apartments! invisible suburbs!
skeleton treasuries! blind capitals! demonic
industries! spectral nations! invincible mad
houses! granite cocks! monstrous bombs!

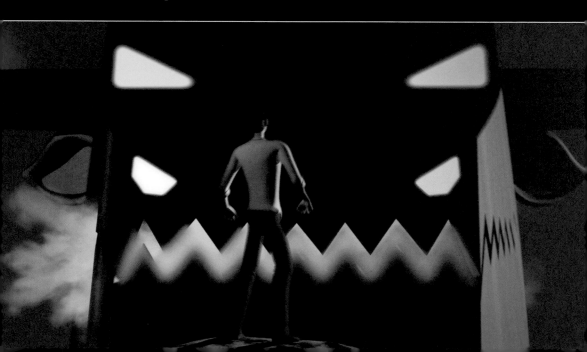

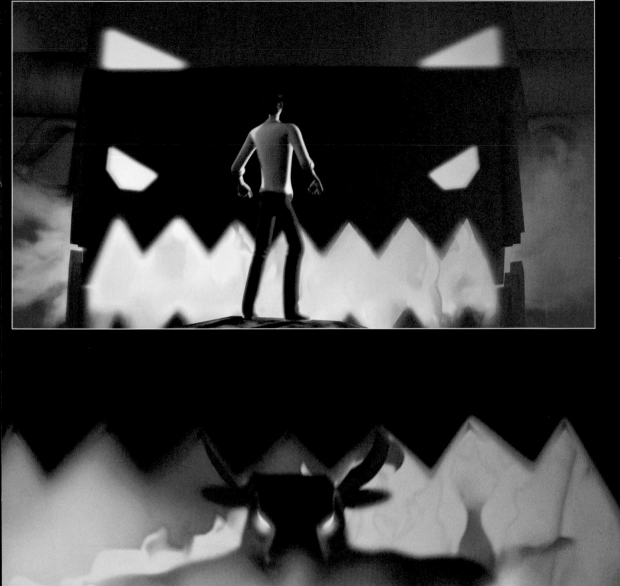

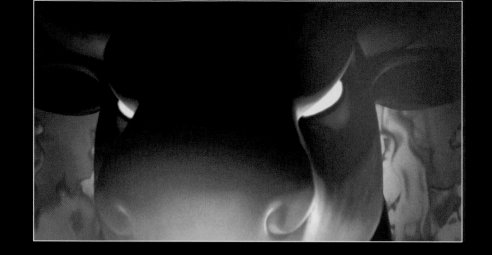

They broke their backs lifting Moloch to Heaven!
Pavements, trees, radios, tons! lifting the city
to Heaven which exists and is everywhere
about us!

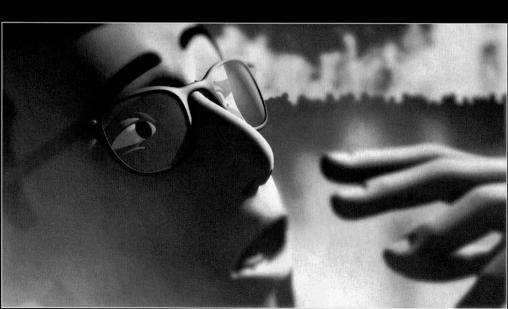

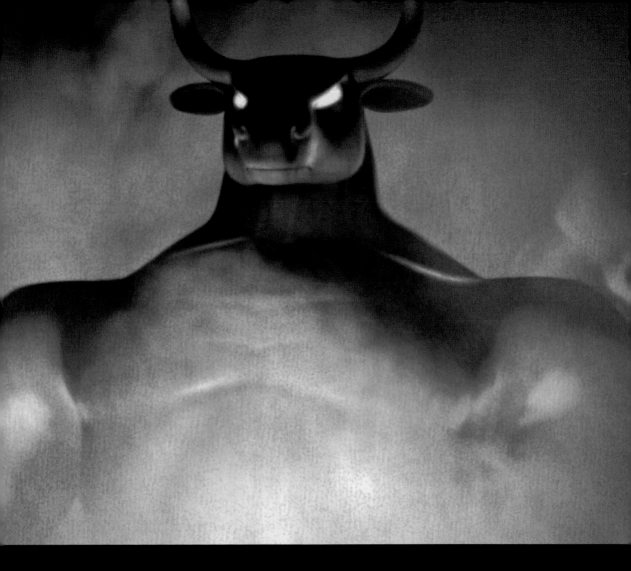

Visions! omens! hallucinations! miracles! ecstasies!
gone down the American river!
Dreams! adorations! illuminations! religions! the
whole boatload of sensitive bullshit!

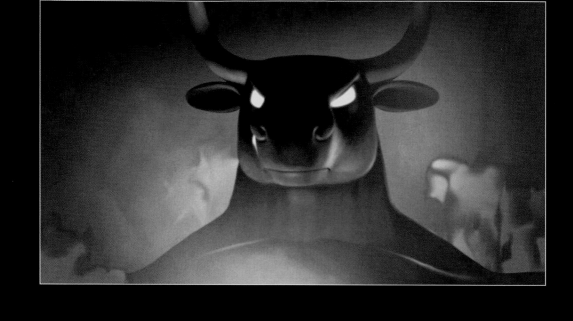

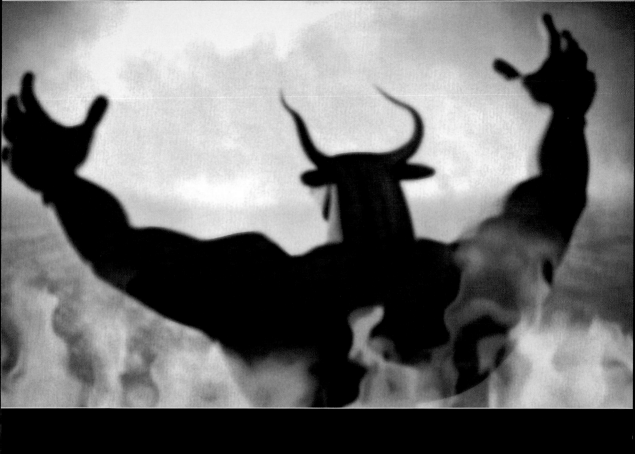

Breakthroughs! over the river! flips and
    crucifixions! gone down the flood! Highs!
    Epiphanies! Despairs! Ten years' animal screams
    and suicides! Minds! New loves! Mad generation!
    down on the rocks of Time!

real holy laughter in the river! They saw it all!
the wild eyes! the holy yells! They bade
farewell! They jumped off the roof! to solitude!
waving! carrying flowers! Down to the river!
into the street!

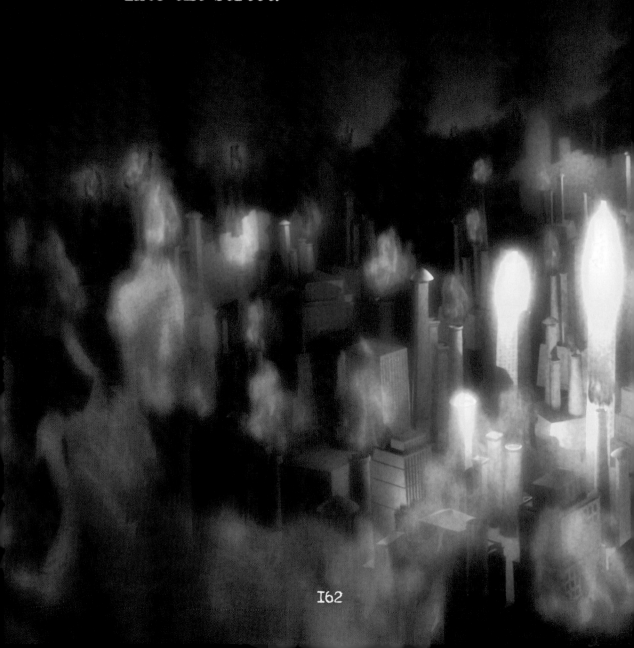

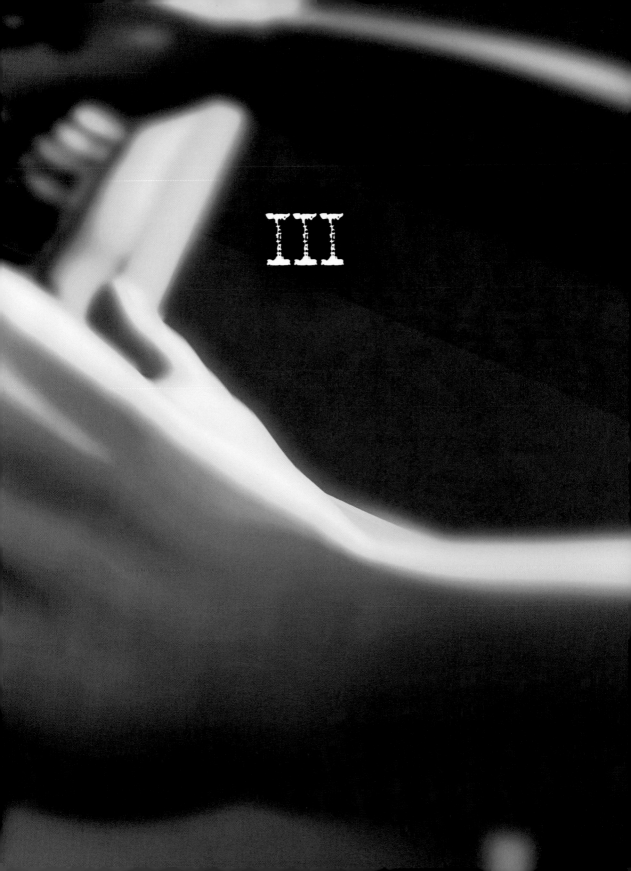

III

Carl Solomon! I'm with you in Rockland where
   you're madder than I am
I'm with you in Rockland where you must feel very
   strange
I'm with you in Rockland where you imitate the
   shade of my mother

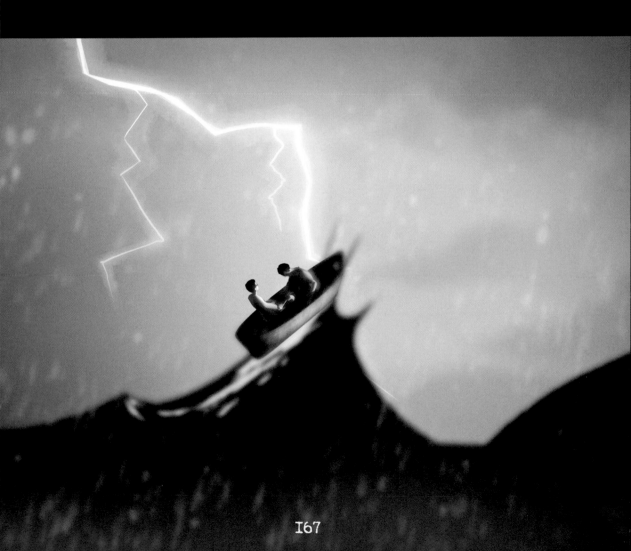

I'm with you in Rockland where you've murdered
    your twelve secretaries
I'm with you in Rockland where you laugh at this
    invisible humor

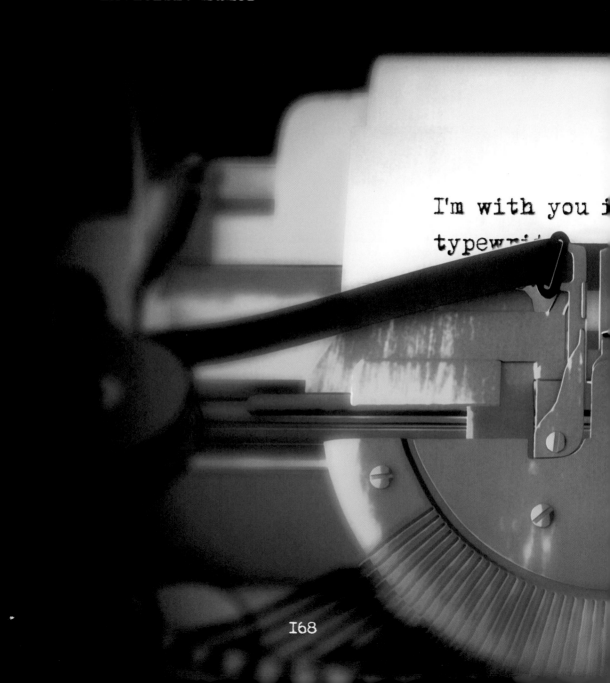

I'm with you i
typewri

I'm with you in Rockland where we are great
writers on the same dreadful typewriter

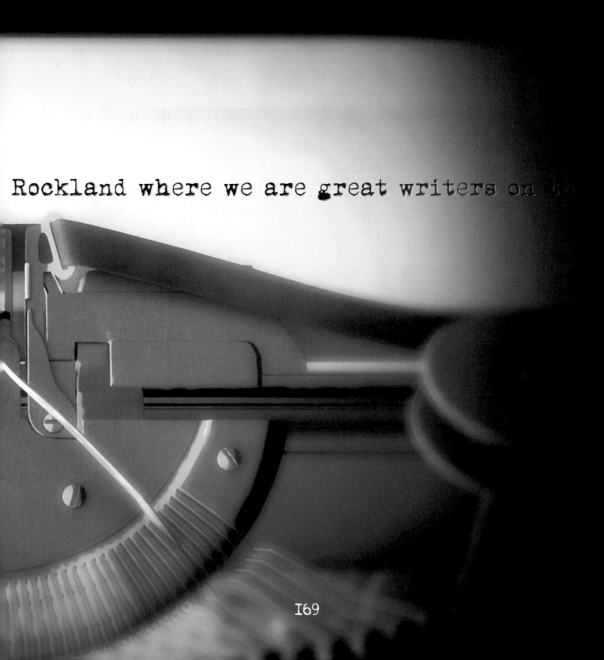

Rockland where we are great writers on

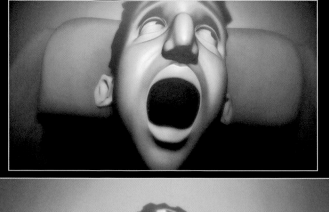

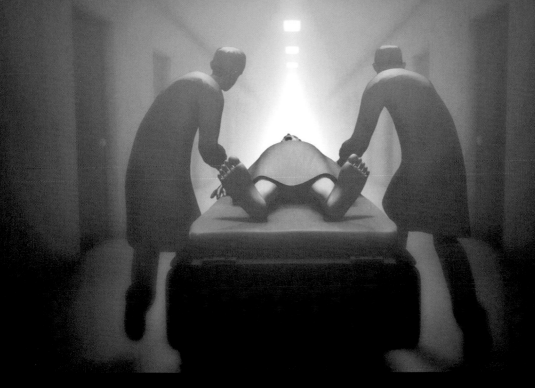

I'm with you in Rockland where your condition
has become serious and is reported on the
radio

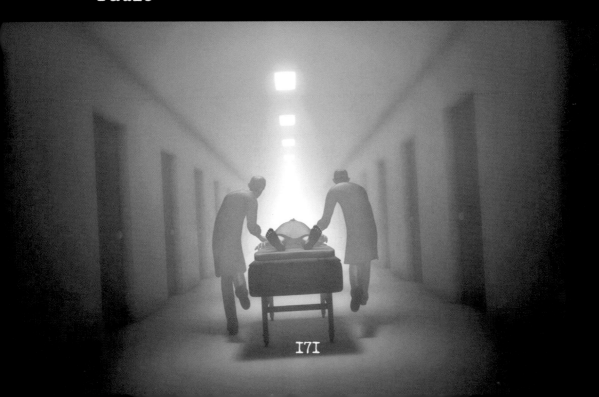

I'm with you in Rockland where the faculties of
the skull no longer admit the worms of the
senses

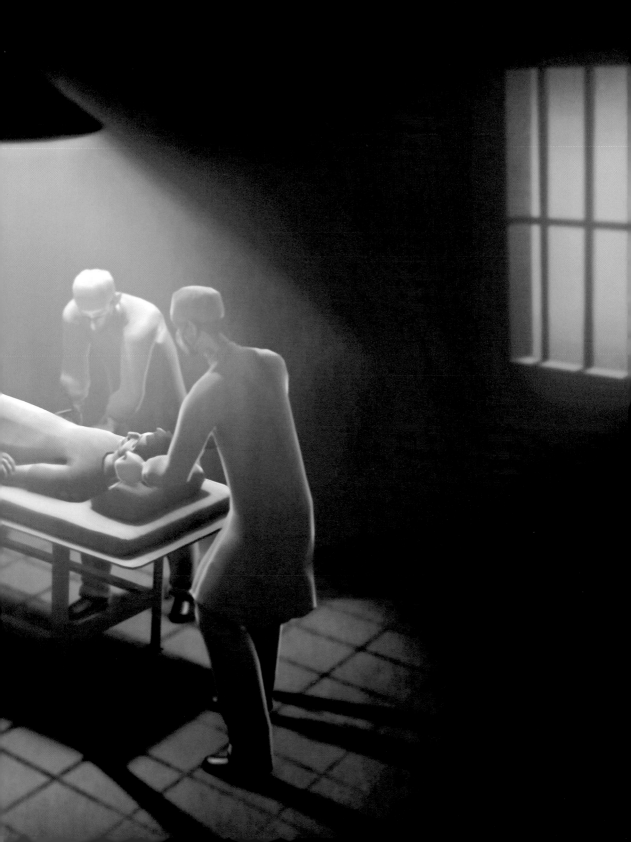

I'm with you in Rockland where you drink the
    tea of the breasts of the spinsters of
    Utica
I'm with you in Rockland where you pun on the
    bodies of your nurses the harpies of the
    Bronx
I'm with you in Rockland where you scream in a
    straightjacket that you're losing the game
    of the actual pingpong of the abyss

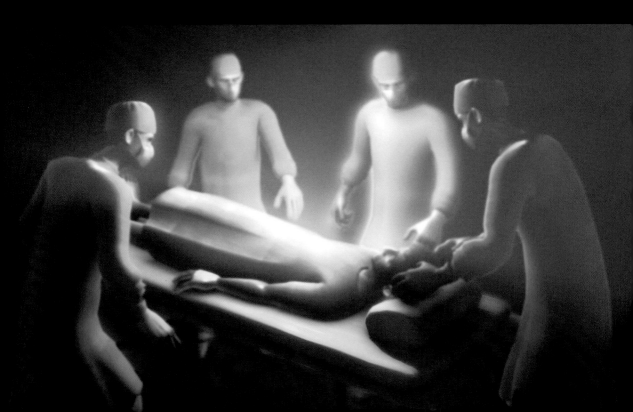

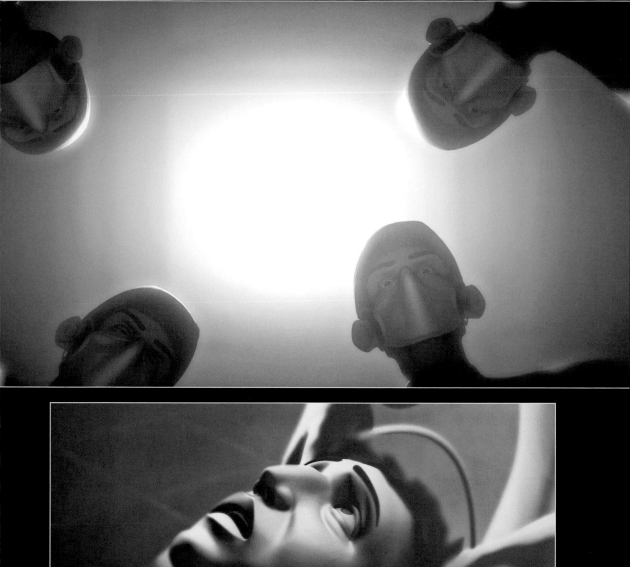

I'm with you in Rockland where you bang on the
    catatonic piano the soul is innocent and
    immortal it should never die ungodly in an
    armed madhouse

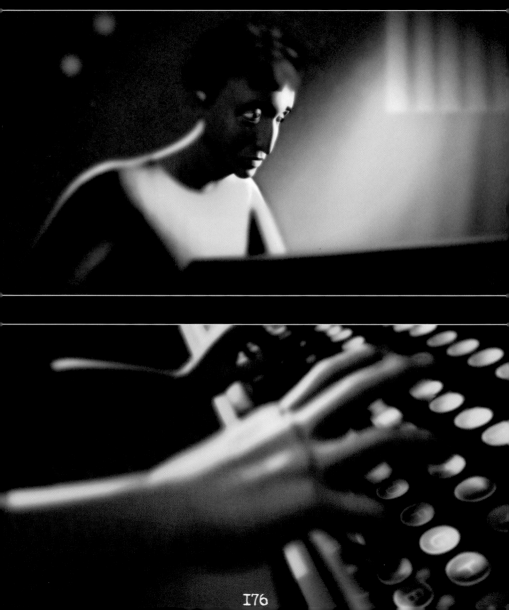

I'm with you in Rockland where fifty more shocks
    will never return your soul to its body again
    from its pilgrimage to a cross in the void

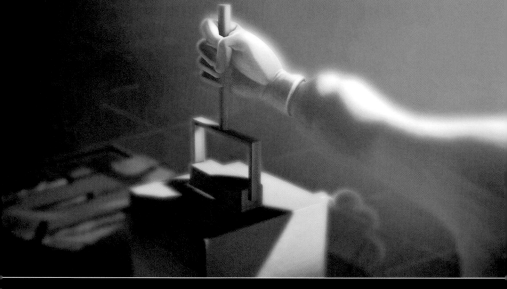

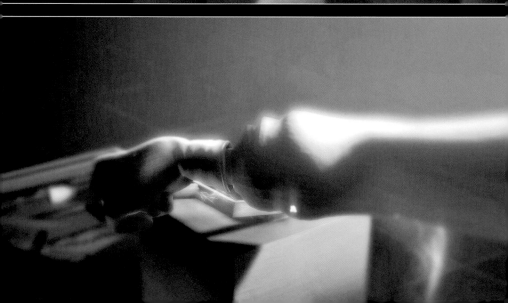

I'm with you in Rockland where you accuse your
    doctors of insanity and plot the Hebrew
    socialist revolution against the fascist
    national Golgotha
I'm with you in Rockland where you will split the
    heavens of Long Island and resurrect your
    living human Jesus from the superhuman tomb

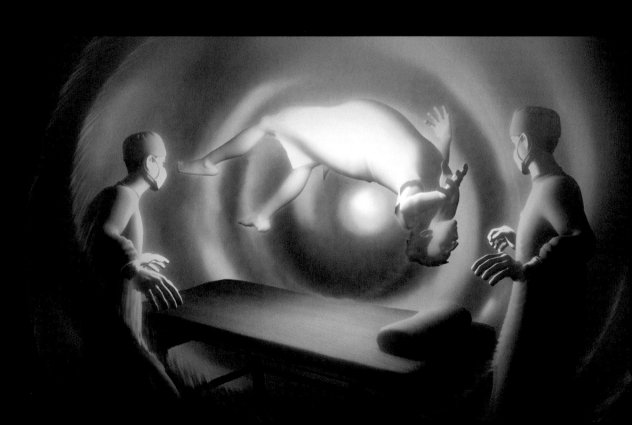

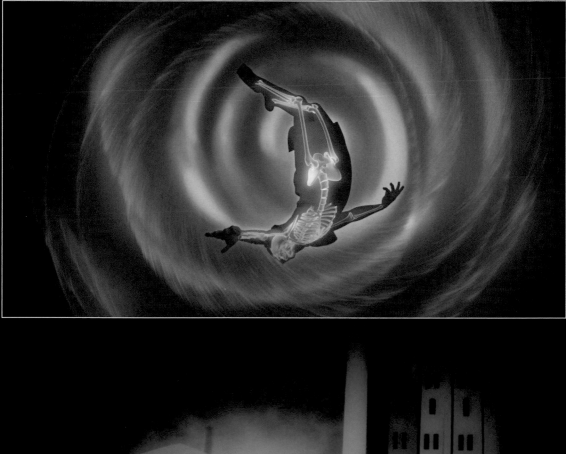

I'm with you in Rockland where there are twenty-
five-thousand mad comrades all together
singing the final stanzas of the
Internationale

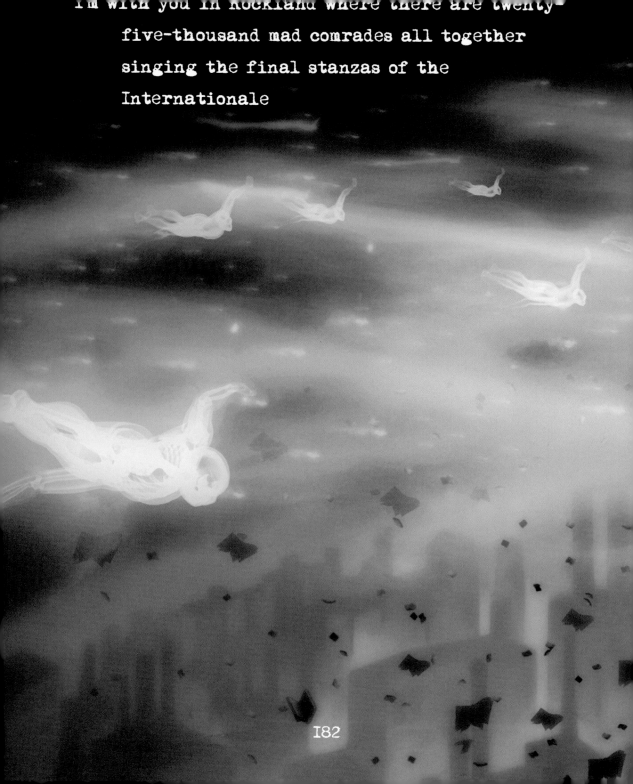

I'm with you in Rockland where we hug and kiss the United States under our bedsheets the United States that coughs all night and won't let us sleep

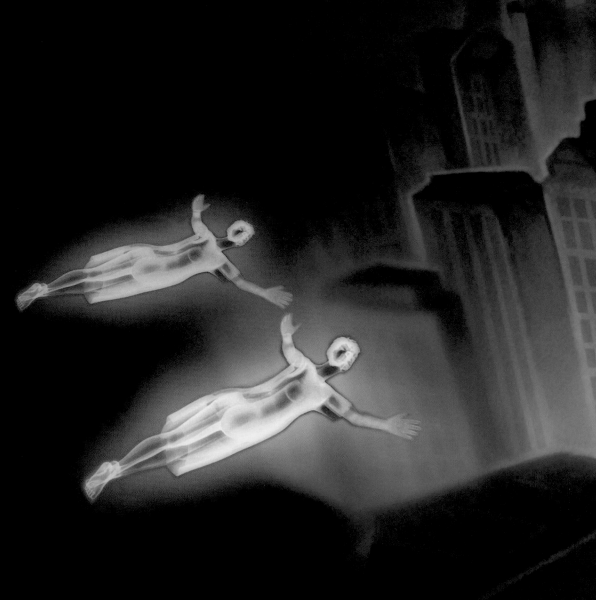

I'm with you in Rockland where we wake up
  electrified out of the coma by our own souls'
  airplanes roaring over the roof . . .

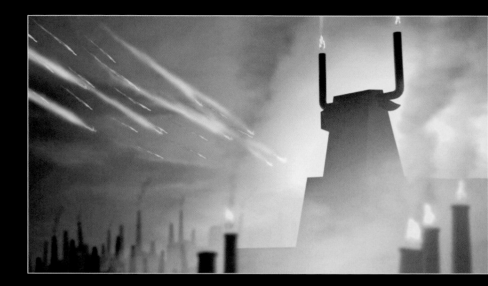

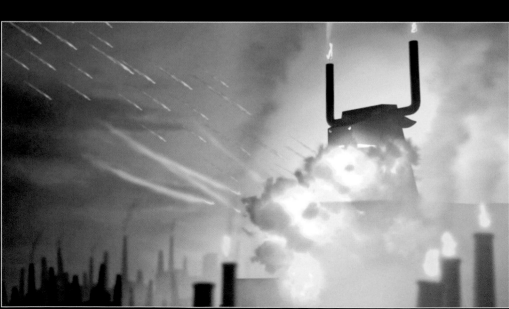

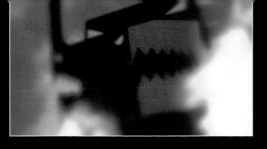
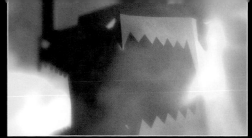

they've come to drop angelic bombs the
hospital illuminates itself imaginary walls
collapse O skinny legions run outside O starry
spangled shock of mercy the eternal war is
here O victory forget your underwear we're
free

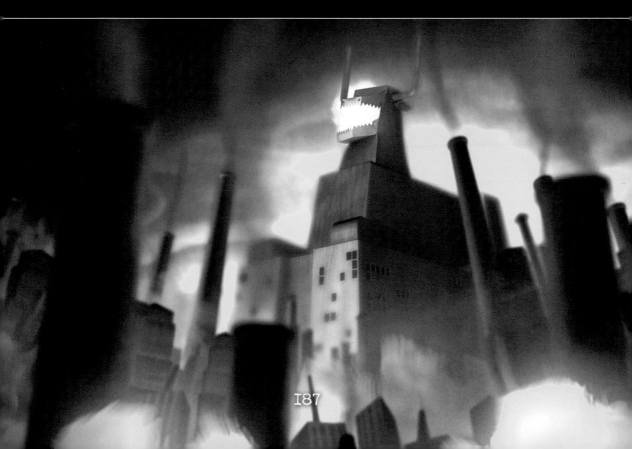

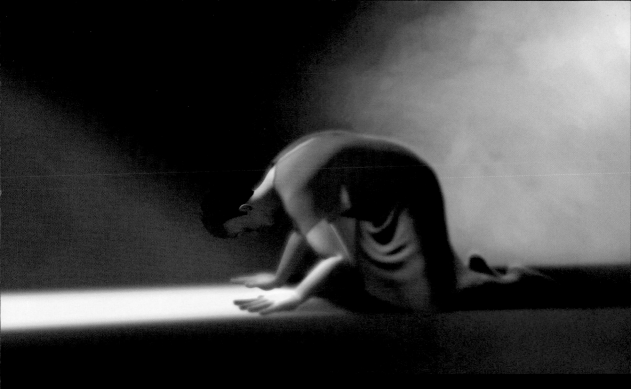

I'm with you in Rockland in my dreams you walk
dripping from a sea-journey on the highway
across America in tears . . .

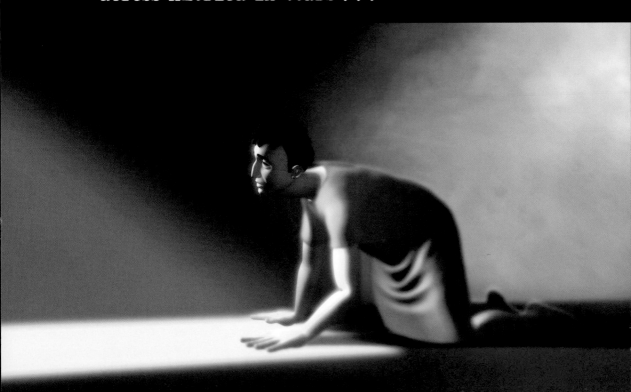

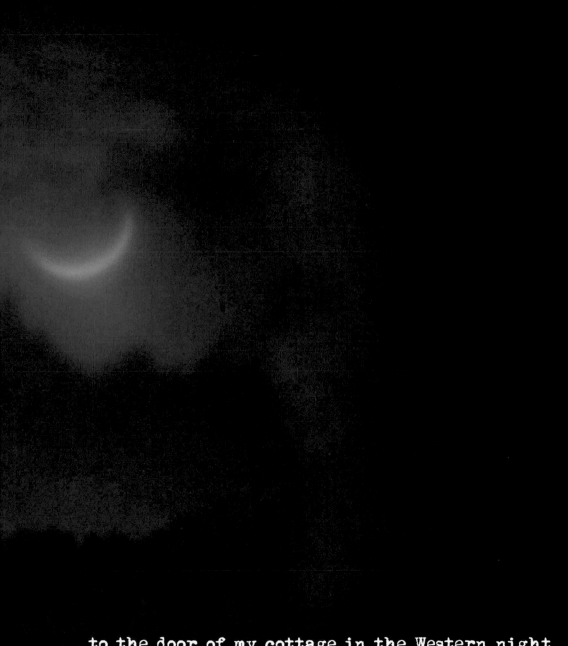

... to the door of my cottage in the Western night

San Francisco, 1955-56

Footnote to
HOWL

Holy! Holy! Holy! Holy! Holy! Holy! Holy! Holy! Holy!
Holy! Holy! Holy! Holy! Holy! Holy!
The world is holy! The soul is holy! The skin is
holy! The nose is holy! The tongue and cock and
hand and asshole holy!

Everything is holy! everybody's holy! everywhere is holy! everyday is in eternity! Everyman's an angel!

The bum's as holy as the seraphim! the madman is holy as you my soul are holy!

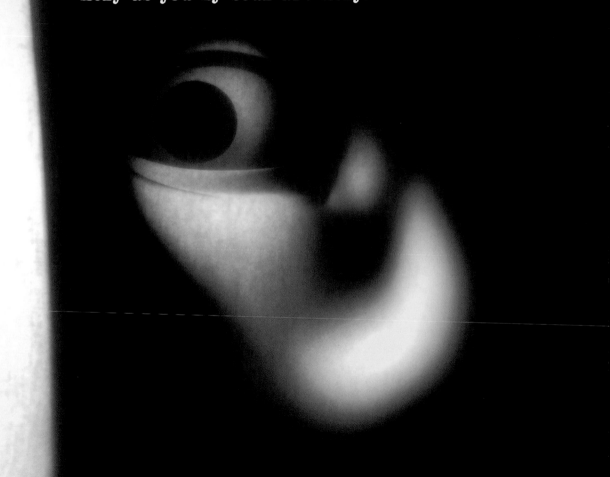

The typewriter is holy the poem is holy the voice
is holy the hearers are holy the ecstasy is
holy!

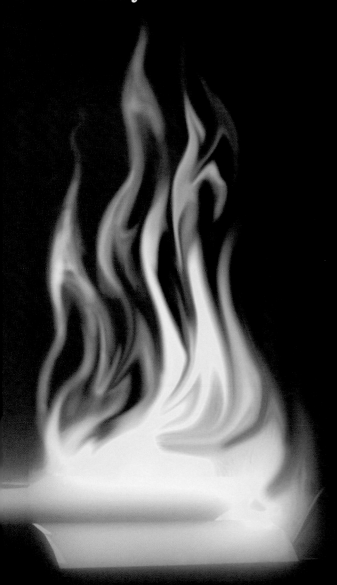

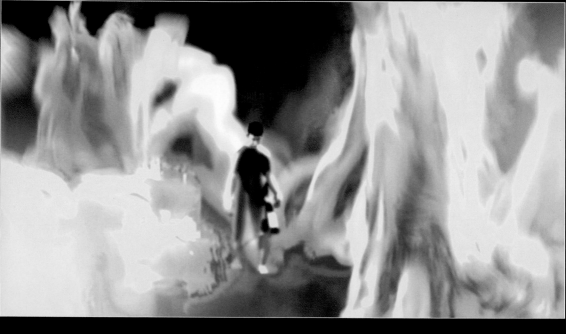

Holy Peter holy Allen holy Solomon holy Lucien
holy Kerouac holy Huncke holy Burroughs
holy Cassady

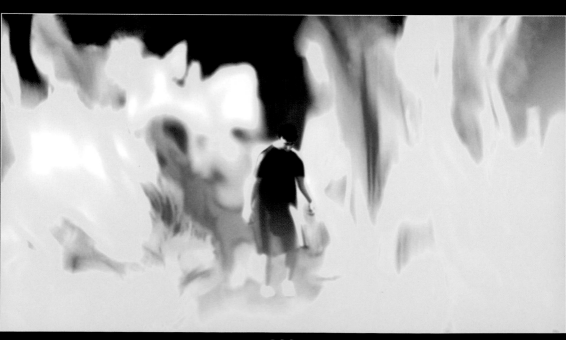

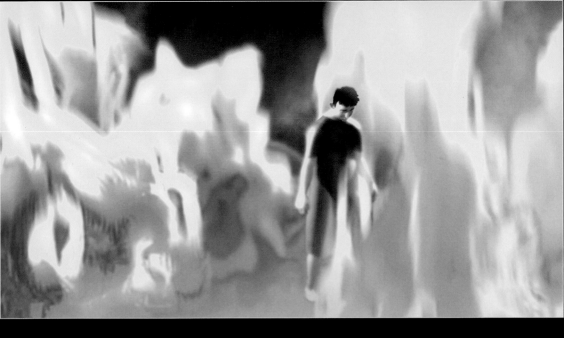

holy the unknown buggered and suffering
beggars holy the hideous human angels!

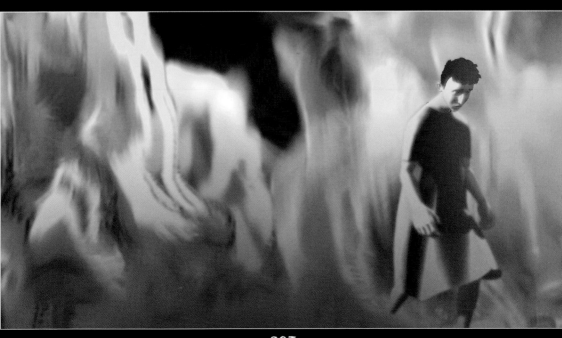

Holy my mother in the insane asylum! Holy the cocks
of the grandfathers of Kansas!

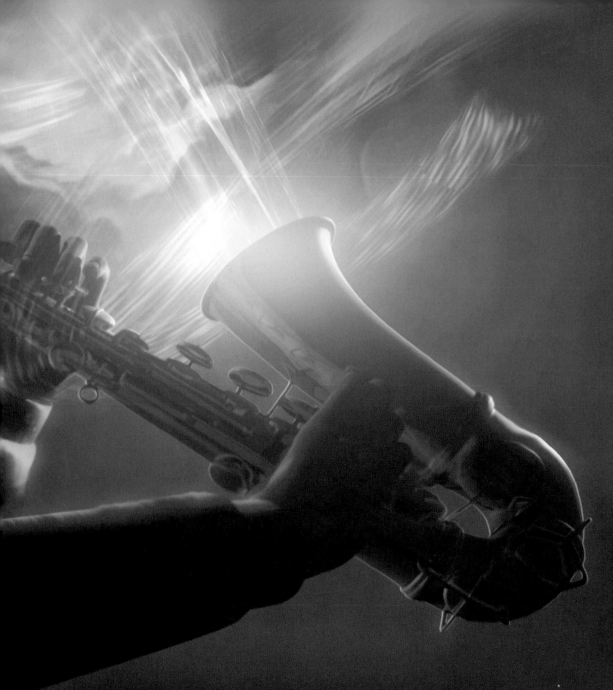

Holy the groaning saxophone! Holy the bop
apocalypse! Holy the jazzbands marijuana
hipsters peace & junk & drums!

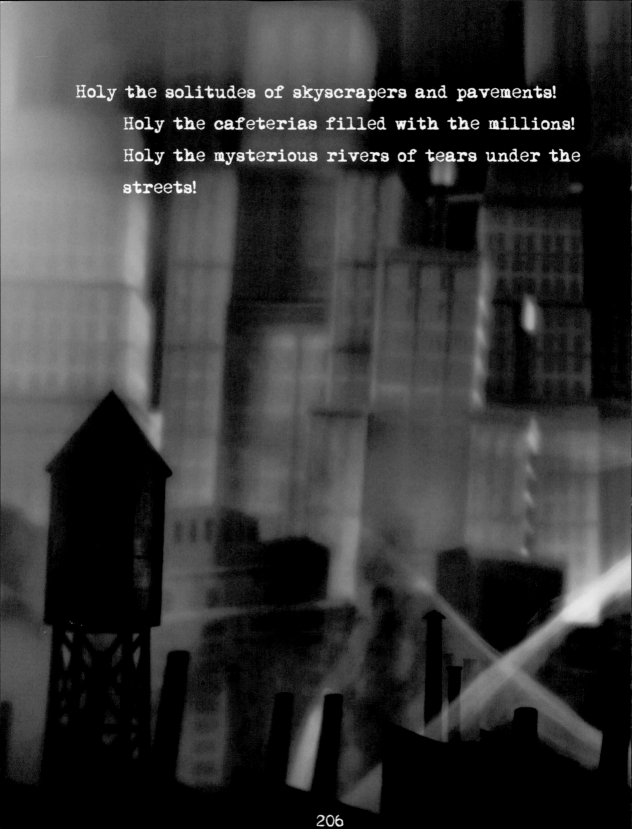

Holy the solitudes of skyscrapers and pavements!
Holy the cafeterias filled with the millions!
Holy the mysterious rivers of tears under the
streets!

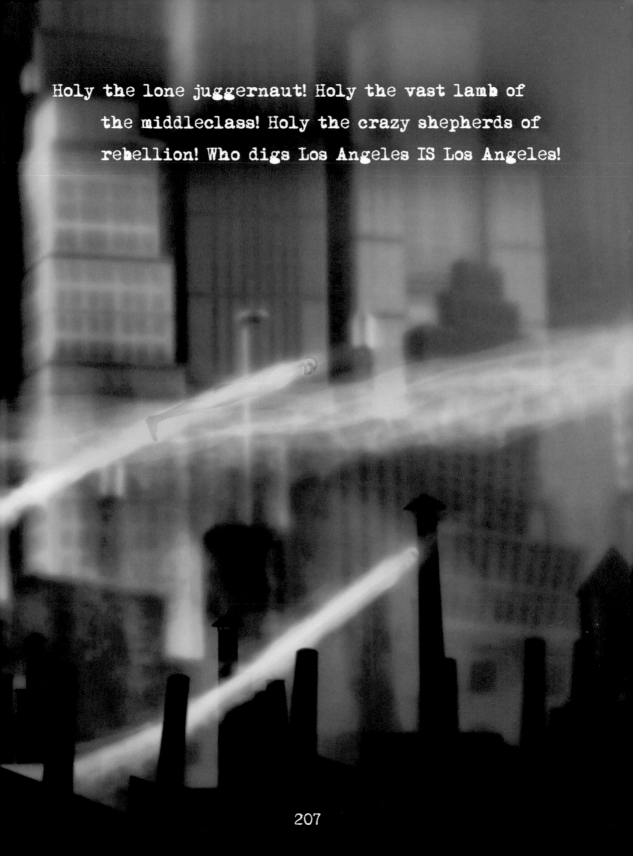

Holy the lone juggernaut! Holy the vast lamb of
the middleclass! Holy the crazy shepherds of
rebellion! Who digs Los Angeles IS Los Angeles!

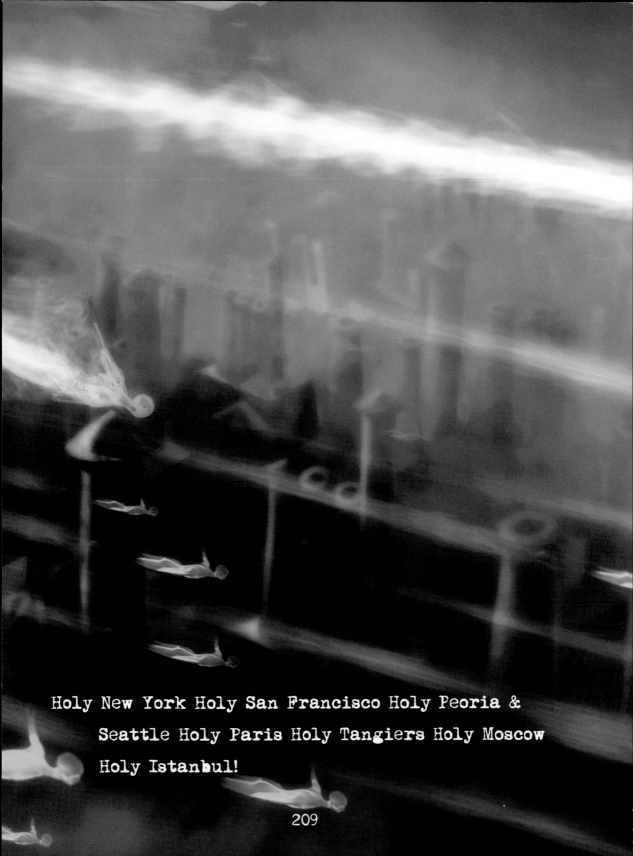

Holy New York Holy San Francisco Holy Peoria &
  Seattle Holy Paris Holy Tangiers Holy Moscow
Holy Istanbul!

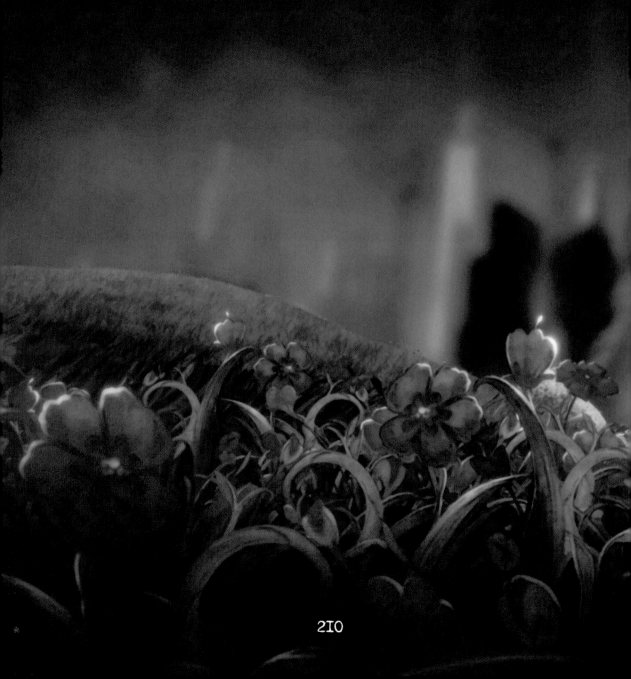

Holy time in eternity holy eternity in time holy
    the clocks in space holy the fourth dimension
    holy the fifth International holy the Angel
    in Moloch!

Holy the sea holy the desert holy the railroad
holy the locomotive holy the visions holy the
hallucinations holy the miracles holy the
eyeball holy the abyss!

Holy forgiveness! mercy! charity! faith! Holy! Ours!
bodies! suffering! magnanimity!

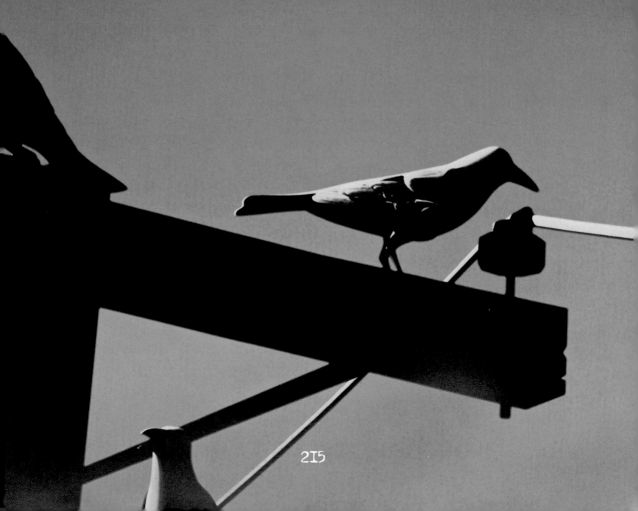

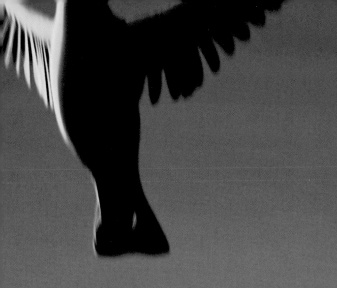

Holy the supernatural extra brilliant intelligent
kindness of the soul!

Berkeley, 1955

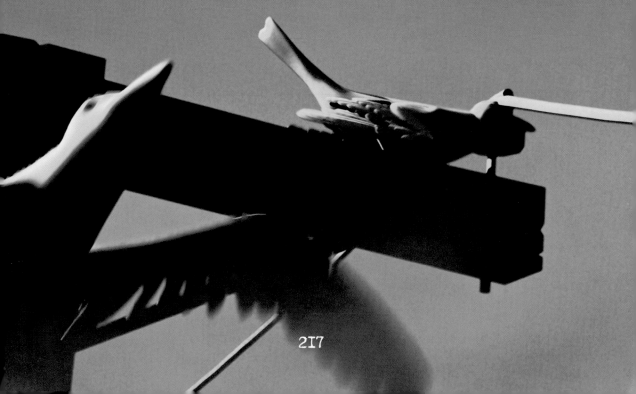

Thunyawat Puna-Ngarm, Chet Jeamkitrung, Chutinart Warunyuwong, Rapipol Koomsup, Ingo Schachner, Sakaret Limsithong, Asawin Konplean, Nat Anuntkosol, Nuttakorn Trivittayakorn.

It was a pleasure to work with folks at HarperCollins; Terry Karten, Lucy Albanese, Susan Kosko, and Amy Baker.

Echoing *thank yous* down the hall to: Jeffrey Posternak & Andrew Wylie, Gus Van Sant, Jawal Nga, David Fenkel, Dan Berger, Gordon Clark, Michael Jantze, Chris Lanier, Tom Rubalcava, Ed Bell, Valentino "Achiu" So, Brian Benson, James Chan, Stan Webb, Kevin N. Bailey, Michael Baker, Allison P. Brown, Michael Ehrenzweig, Mark Steele, Geoff Sass, Lippy, Nina Paley, Eliot Katz, Danny Schechter, Stephan Ielpi, Peter Orlovsky, Lawrence Ferlinghetti, Tuli Kupferberg, Hal & Nina . . . and Emma & Maya.

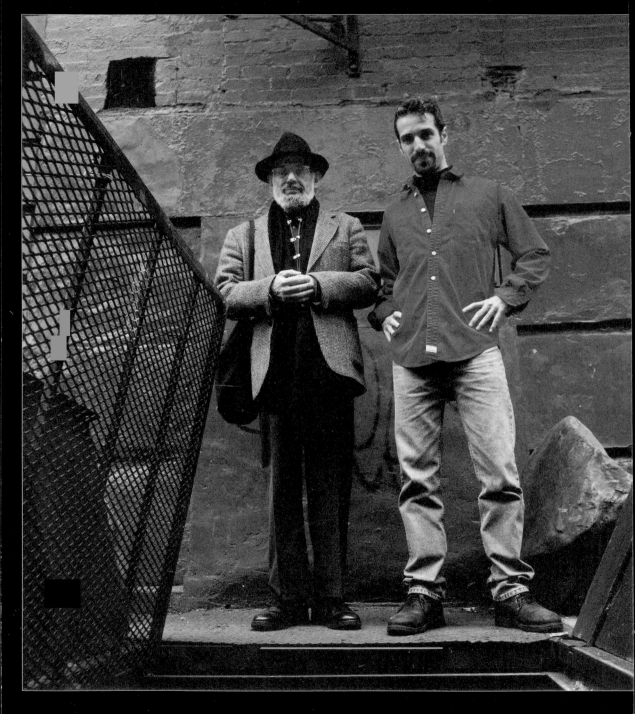

Allen Ginsberg and Eric Drooker on the Lower East Side of New York City, 1996.